Master the Science of Miracles®

The Reliable, Repeatable, Step-by-Step System
For Transforming Your Thoughts Into Your Reality

by Ron Matthews

i

ISBN: 979-8-9929858-0-1
Cover and interior design by Ron Matthews
Printed by Amazon KDP
First edition

Visit: www.MasterTheScienceOfMiracles.com

For the seekers,
the dreamers,
and those who yearn
to remember who they truly are.

For my wife, Diane—
The love of my life,
the quiet light behind every miracle,
and the one I get to walk beside,
every day of this extraordinary life.

For my son, Jason—
test subject #1,
lifelong friend,
and proof that miracles run in the family.

"Everything in the universe is within you. Ask all from yourself."
— Rúmí

"The Reality of man is his thought, not his material body."
—'Abdu'l-Bahá

Disclaimer

This book is intended for informational and educational purposes only. It is not intended to diagnose, treat, cure, or prevent any physical, mental, or emotional condition, nor is it a substitute for professional medical, psychological, or psychiatric advice or care.

The author shares insights and methods based on personal experience, research, and spiritual practice. While every effort has been made to ensure the accuracy and effectiveness of the information presented, no guarantees are made regarding specific results or outcomes.

Readers are encouraged to consult with qualified healthcare or mental health professionals before making any changes to their health, wellness, or lifestyle practices. The author disclaims any liability arising directly or indirectly from the use or application of the contents of this book.

By reading this book, you agree to take full responsibility for your choices, your energy, and your personal growth journey.

Table of Contents

Acknowledgments

In bringing this work to you, I am standing on the shoulders of giants. These giants include such luminaries such as...

- 'Abdu'l-Bahá
- Jalál ad-Dín Muhammad Rúmí
- Max Freedom Long
- José Silva
- Donna Eden
- Raymon Grace
- C.W. Leadbeater

Chapter 1: Awakening the Miraculous Power Within

Section 1 – A Personal Miracle: Healing from Glaucoma

Every great system begins with a story—and this one begins with a personal miracle.

Years ago, I sat in a doctor's office hearing words no one wants to hear: *"Your intraocular pressure is dangerously high. If this continues, you'll lose your vision."* The diagnosis was glaucoma. The prognosis, according to every expert, was eventual blindness.

But somewhere deep inside me, a quiet, unwavering voice said: *No.* Not out of denial. Not out of fear. But from a place beyond reason—a place that knew something else was possible.

I didn't reject medical treatment. I took the prescribed eye drops as directed. But I also turned to what I knew from decades of studying energy, consciousness, and inner transformation. I treated the condition not as a fixed reality but as a **temporary expression of internal imbalance**—a manifestation that could be redirected through alignment of thought, energy, and intention.

Day by day, I practiced what would eventually become part of the MSM system:
✓ Focused thought-forms charged with elevated emotion
✓ Directing energy through the hands and breath
✓ Rewriting subconscious beliefs around decline, aging, and inevitability

On my next visit to the eye doctor a month later, my intraocular pressure was **completely normal**. The same doctors who warned me about blindness had no explanation. But I did.

1

This wasn't just spontaneous healing. This was a **repeatable result**, born of inner work and spiritual alignment. And while it may sound extraordinary, I discovered something even more powerful:

It was not a fluke. It was a formula.

What began as an act of personal necessity became a path of discovery. I began to test and refine the exact steps I had taken—identifying what worked, what didn't, and what produced consistent results when shared with others.

That process, born from the tension between fear and faith, would grow into something much larger than a healing protocol. It would become *Master the Science of Miracles®*—a comprehensive system for transforming not only the body, but every area of life where limitation had once been accepted as fact.

This book is not a memoir of that healing—it is the blueprint that emerged from it.

And it begins here.

Section 2 – The Reality of Thought and Belief

Most people walk through life under the impression that reality is fixed—that what happens around them is the result of circumstances, genetics, or sheer luck. But in truth, **reality bends to belief**, especially the beliefs we don't realize we hold.

The subconscious self does not distinguish between truth and falsehood, between what is possible and what is not. It responds to **what is repeated, emotionally charged, and accepted as real**—whether that reality is empowering or destructive.

This is why *Master the Science of Miracles®* begins with **the inner landscape**, not the outer world. Because the life you're living now is the result of seeds planted long ago in the garden of your subconscious. Some of those seeds were lovingly placed there—values, dreams, aspirations. Others were dropped by accident, or even imposed by others—doubt, shame, fear, scarcity.

If your subconscious mind is a garden, then your beliefs are the roots of every visible outcome in your life.

You cannot harvest joy from seeds of unworthiness.
You cannot grow abundance from roots tangled in fear.
You cannot reap peace if your soil is saturated with self-judgment.

But here's the liberating truth: **you can replant.**
You can become the gardener of your own subconscious reality.

That's where this system begins—by helping you become aware of the hidden beliefs and emotional patterns that have shaped your life, and giving you the tools to **pull up what no longer serves you** and plant something higher, something aligned, something miraculous.

In MSM, we don't just "think positive." We work with the subconscious self in its native language—**emotion, sensation, imagery, and repetition**—to form new thought-forms so vivid and charged that they override the old programming and take root as living, energetic realities.

This is not a metaphor. It's not wishful thinking. It is a **replicable science of transformation** that begins with the way you think and feel—and ends with the way your life unfolds.

In the next section, I'll share how this path evolved—not in theory, but in practice—through decades of personal experimentation with ancient and modern systems of transformation, until the pieces came together into the unified framework you now hold in your hands.

Section 3 – The MSM Origin Story

The system you're about to learn wasn't handed to me in a single flash of insight. It wasn't channeled. It wasn't downloaded. It was **discovered**—piece by piece, step by step, over decades of study, practice, failure, and breakthrough.

Long before I called it *Master the Science of Miracles®*, I was testing everything I could find. I studied spiritual traditions, healing modalities, mental training systems, and metaphysical practices—some of which were preserved in ancient texts, and others passed through oral traditions or obscured by time.

I worked with shamanic principles, Eastern energy arts, Western psychology, and modern mind-body science. Some methods produced real, tangible results. Others left me skeptical or searching for what was missing.

But whenever something worked—whenever a process yielded transformation in myself or others—I didn't just celebrate. I **reverse-engineered it**. I asked:

- What were the exact mental, emotional, and energetic components involved?

- What was the mechanism of action—seen or unseen?

- Could this be repeated, scaled, taught?

One by one, these scattered tools and concepts began to **connect**. What once looked like isolated techniques revealed themselves to be **fragments of a larger pattern**—like pieces of a puzzle pointing toward a complete system.

Eventually, the principles sorted themselves into an elegant structure. Not a loose collection of techniques, but a fully integrated system that **bridged the conscious, subconscious, and Transcendent Selves**, and could be applied to **any area of life**.

When I began teaching it to others, the feedback was immediate and profound. People reported breakthroughs in areas where they had been stuck for years. Those who followed the steps with sincerity and consistency experienced shifts that felt miraculous—but were, in truth, the predictable outcome of energetic alignment.

And that's when I knew this needed a name. I wanted something that honored both the **mystery** and the **method**. Something that reflected the awe of divine co-creation and the precision of an applied discipline.

The name came simply and clearly: *Master the Science of Miracles*®.

And the people who experienced the deepest results? They weren't the most experienced or "spiritual." They were simply the most **compliant**—meaning they showed up, followed the steps, and allowed the system to work.

This book is for those ready to do the same. You don't have to believe everything at once. You don't have to be perfect. But if you stay with the process and work the system, the system will work you—in the best way possible.

In the next section, I'll explain why so many powerful systems of transformation seem to work partially—or not at all—and why MSM was designed to **integrate what others have only isolated**.

Section 4 – The Blind Men and the Elephant: A Parable of Fragmented Understanding

You may be familiar with the ancient parable of the blind men and the elephant. In the story, a group of blind men are brought to an elephant for the first time and asked to describe what it is. Each man touches a different part of the animal—one the tusk, another the ear, another the tail—and each confidently declares what he believes the elephant to be.

"To me," says one, "an elephant is like a spear."
"No," says another, "it's clearly like a fan."
"You're both wrong," insists a third, "it's obviously like a rope."

They aren't wrong—but they aren't right either. They're each grasping **a partial truth**, mistaking it for the whole.

This story is more than a parable—it's a **perfect metaphor** for the world of personal transformation. Over the years, I've watched people devote themselves to one tool or one modality, convinced they've found the answer, only to hit a wall when it stops working or fails to deliver consistent results.

5

They touch one part of the elephant and say, "This is it." But without understanding the **whole system**, their progress is partial, their results inconsistent, and their frustration inevitable.

Consider just a few of the most common "pieces" people cling to:

- **Law of Attraction** teachings emphasize mental focus and emotional vibration—but often leave people discouraged when unhealed blocks prevent manifestation.

- **Meditative practices** like Silva UltraMind or other alpha-state techniques guide the mind into receptive states—but don't always show how to sustain emotional alignment.

- **Energy systems** such as Qigong, Yoga, and Reiki develop internal power—but don't clearly link that power to thought-form creation.

- **Secular goal-setting methods** focus on clarity and action—but frequently ignore the energetic and subconscious dimensions.

- **Traditional and indigenous prayer forms** tap into spiritual connection—but often rely on blind faith without a conscious understanding of inner mechanics.

Each of these is a powerful part of the puzzle. But each, on its own, is incomplete.

Just like the blind men, each approach touches truth—but misses the totality of what's possible.

What's needed isn't more parts. What's needed is a **framework** that brings the parts together.

And that's exactly what *Master the Science of Miracles*® is.

In the next section, we'll explore how MSM emerged as that integrative framework—one that unites the best of what other systems offer, and empowers you to use **all your faculties**, aligned and activated, to create true transformation.

Section 5 – One Elephant, Many Parts: Toward Integration

For transformation to be lasting, effective, and aligned with your true nature, it must be **whole**. That means it must address the full spectrum of what makes you human: your thoughts, your emotions, your energy, and your spiritual essence.

The reason so many systems feel incomplete is because they focus on one part of the elephant—mental focus, emotional regulation, physical energy, or spiritual devotion—without understanding how these elements interact.

Master the Science of Miracles® is not another piece of the puzzle. It is the **frame that holds the puzzle together**, giving you a step-by-step system to awaken, align, and activate the **entire triune nature of your being**.

✓ It trains the **conscious self** to shape desire into a focused intention.
✓ It teaches the **subconscious self** to energize that intention and deliver it in the right language.
✓ It opens the pathway to the **Transcendent Self**, the most exalted part of you, so the desire can be fulfilled in accordance with the highest good.

MSM is designed to **integrate** the very best of what works in modern neuroscience, ancient spiritual systems, energy work, and psychological insight. But it doesn't stop there. It shows you **how to use these tools together**, in harmony, and in the right sequence.

Integration is what transforms scattered potential into creative power.

Instead of trying to balance multiple disconnected practices—or worse, giving up when one doesn't work—MSM offers you a **reliable, repeatable, and holistic framework** that brings every part of you online.

The result? A system that's not only effective, but elegant. One that feels like a return—not to something new, but to something ancient and familiar. Something that's always been inside you, waiting to be awakened.

7

In the next section, we'll begin unpacking the foundational principle that makes this possible: the triune nature of the human being.

Section 6 – The Triune Nature of the Human Being

If you've ever sensed that there's more to you than your thoughts... more than your body... more than your emotions... you're right.

In MSM, we work with a foundational understanding that the human being is not a single self, but a **triune being** composed of three distinct and cooperative aspects:

1. **The Conscious Self**

2. **The Subconscious Self**

3. **The Transcendent Self**

This model is not a modern invention. It is rooted in ancient teachings and confirmed through the work of observers, shamans, psychologists, and spiritual seekers across time and cultures.

Max Freedom Long—whose early 20th-century research into Hawaiian spiritual practice helped reintroduce this triune model to the West—called these three aspects the Low Self, Middle Self, and High Self. MSM uses updated language to reflect their function more accurately: **subconscious**, **conscious**, and **Transcendent**.

Carl Jung, too, recognized something similar. His concepts of the ego, the personal unconscious, and the collective unconscious echoed this structure, though described through a different lens. Other systems speak of body, mind, and spirit. Still others refer to the self, the soul, and the divine. These are all variations on the same profound insight:

Human beings are **multi-layered**, and miracles only occur when those layers work in alignment.

Throughout this book, you'll see how each of the three selves plays a vital role—not just in your healing or manifestation journey, but in your very capacity to live a fulfilling life.

In the next section, we'll look more closely at the unique characteristics of each self, and how they interact to create your inner and outer reality.

Section 7 – Understanding the Three Selves

To truly work the *Master the Science of Miracles®* system, you must do more than accept the existence of the three selves—you must **learn to work with each one directly**, in the language it understands, and in the role it was designed to play.

Let's take a closer look at each:

The Conscious Self

This is the "you" most people identify with—the one who thinks, plans, decides, and evaluates. It is the seat of logic, reason, and language. It is capable of imagining a better life, setting goals, and making choices.

But here's the challenge: the conscious self **cannot manifest anything on its own**. It can conceive of a goal, but it cannot bring it into being without help. It relies entirely on the subconscious and Transcendent Selves to **carry and fulfill its desires**.

The Subconscious Self

This self is the engine room of your being. It governs your memories, emotions, habits, and bodily functions. It holds every experience you've ever had—along with the beliefs, traumas, and energetic patterns that grew out of them.

The subconscious self is **literal, emotional, and impressionable**. It believes whatever is repeated with feeling, whether or not it's true.

9

That's why affirmations can fail if they don't reach the subconscious in a language it trusts.

Importantly, the subconscious self is the **sole channel** through which the conscious self can communicate with the Transcendent Self. If this channel is clear, miracles flow. If it's blocked by unresolved emotion or limiting beliefs, progress stalls.

The Transcendent Self

This is your highest self—eternal, divine, and unbound by space or time. It is the part of you that **knows without thinking**, that **loves without condition**, and that **creates without limitation**.

You cannot command or manipulate the Transcendent Self. But you can communicate with it—**through the subconscious self**, using a special kind of emotionally-charged message called a **multi-sensory thought-form** (explored in detail later).

When all three selves are aligned—when the conscious self focuses, the subconscious self energizes, and the Transcendent Self receives— **miracles become not only possible but predictable**.

MSM is the method that brings this alignment into your everyday life.

In the final section of this introduction, you'll see why this triune structure is not just theoretical—it's the key to the transformation you've been seeking, and the reason this system works when others don't.

Section 8 – Aligning the Three Selves: The Purpose of MSM

Now that you understand the distinct roles of the conscious self, subconscious self, and Transcendent Self, you can begin to see why many personal growth systems fall short. They may speak to the mind, or stir the emotions, or open the heart—but **rarely do they align all three**.

That's the purpose of *Master the Science of Miracles®*.

This system doesn't ask you to choose between science and spirituality, logic and feeling, action and surrender. It weaves them together—**not as conflicting forces, but as cooperative aspects of your own being.**

When properly aligned:

- The conscious self **focuses the vision**

- The subconscious self **energizes and transmits the vision**

- The Transcendent Self **transforms the vision into reality**

And this process can be taught. Practiced. Mastered.

It's not unlike what the Rig Veda pointed to thousands of years ago—the idea that **pure consciousness** gives rise to all phenomena. When the individual mind aligns with that universal field, transformation occurs not by chance, but by law.

MSM makes this ancient wisdom **practical, structured, and repeatable**.

The system you're about to learn will show you:

- How to work with the subconscious self using the language it understands

- How to clear inner resistance and reprogram limiting beliefs

- How to construct vivid, emotionally-charged thought-forms that reach the Transcendent Self

- How to activate the energy of miracles and direct it through the heart

This is not theory. It is **the blueprint I've lived**, and the same system that has produced life-changing results for those who commit to it with sincerity.

So let's begin. Not with blind hope, but with confidence.

Because when you align the full power of who you are, the miraculous becomes **your new normal**.

Chapter 2: Overview of the MSM System

Section 1 – Unlocking Your Hidden Potential

Imagine this: You're standing at the edge of a vast, untouched landscape. The air hums with possibility, the horizon stretching endlessly before you. You sense something **just beyond your reach**, an unseen force waiting for you to tap into it.

This is not just **wishful thinking**—it's **reality**. There is a profound intelligence, a guiding presence that has been walking beside you your entire life, **whispering insights, nudging you toward your highest potential**. Most people dismiss these moments of intuition or inspiration, chalking them up to coincidence. But what if they weren't?

What if there was a way to **consciously connect** with this force? To receive **clear guidance**, to create outcomes in a structured and repeatable way, to step into a reality where life flows in your favor?

That's exactly what **Master the Science of Miracles®** is designed to do.

At its core, **MSM** is not about **blind faith or positive thinking**. It's about unlocking the mechanics behind **real transformation**—the same mechanics that spiritual traditions, mystical lineages, and cutting-edge scientific research have been pointing to for centuries. It's about **tapping into the unseen forces that shape reality** and learning how to work with them, rather than against them.

And here's the best part: **You are not doing this alone.**

There is a **collective intelligence**—a network of enlightened guides, mentors, and teachers—available to you at all times. They exist **at the level of your own High Self**, beyond the reach of ordinary perception but ready to assist you the moment you engage them in the right way.

Master the Science of Miracles® is your bridge to that **higher intelligence**. It is a system built from the wisdom of ancient spiritual traditions, the precision of modern methodologies like NLP and energy psychology, and the **lost knowledge of how the human mind, body, and spirit truly function together**.

For some, these concepts may feel **new or even radical**. But for those who have sensed there is more—more to themselves, more to life, more to what is possible—this is **the missing piece** they've been searching for.

You are about to **reawaken abilities that have always been within you**, waiting to be activated. This journey is not about adding something **new** to yourself—it's about remembering who you were **before the world told you otherwise**.

The process you're about to learn will challenge you, expand you, and most importantly, **empower you**. But it requires something from you first—**an open mind and a willingness to step beyond the limitations you've been taught to accept as reality**.

Are you ready?

Because once you see what you are truly capable of, **there's no going back.**

Section 2 – Breaking Free from the Status Quo

You were never meant to live a **small** life.

Yet, from the moment you were born, you were **trained to forget** who you really are.

Society, education, media, and even well-meaning family members told you that the world operates by a fixed set of rules—rules that define what is *real* and what is *impossible.* They taught you to believe that success requires **endless struggle**, that miracles belong to ancient myths, and that your ability to shape reality is limited to what you can see and touch.

But what if those limitations weren't *truth*, but *conditioning*?

What if the extraordinary abilities described in ancient texts, the so-called "supernatural" feats performed by mystics and shamans, were not the stuff of **fairy tales**, but echoes of a power **you still possess**?

The Illusion of Limitation

For generations, people have been **conditioned to doubt their own potential**. Anyone who speaks of intuition, energy, or unseen forces is dismissed as irrational. Even when undeniable evidence emerges—stories of spontaneous healings, near-death experiences, unexplainable synchronicities—society brushes them off as coincidence or delusion.

But beneath the surface, people *know* the truth.

A **nationwide poll** cited in the **National Science Foundation's** 2002 report asked a simple question:

"Do you believe that some people possess psychic powers or ESP?"

An astonishing **60% of Americans** said *yes*.

And the most fascinating part? The **more educated the person was, the more likely they were to believe in these abilities.**

- Among those without a high school diploma, **46%** believed in ESP.

- Among those with a **college education**, that number **jumped to 62%**.

- And among the "attentive public" (those who actively seek knowledge and stay informed), the belief rate soared to **nearly 60%**.

Clearly, belief in human potential **doesn't stem from ignorance—it grows stronger with knowledge**.

The more people explore, question, and seek, the more they begin to sense what has always been true: **We are far more powerful than we've been led to believe.**

15

People aren't rejecting science. They're rejecting a **narrow definition of reality**—one that dismisses **anything that can't be measured with a ruler or dissected under a microscope**.

Reclaiming Your Power
Right now, you are standing at a crossroads.

On one side is **the life you were taught to accept**—a life where you must struggle, where your dreams are "unrealistic," where miracles are things that happen *to* you, not things you create.

On the other side is a **life of limitless potential**—a life where you awaken the abilities that have always been within you, where you work in harmony with the unseen forces that shape reality, where success and fulfillment flow effortlessly because you've learned how to *align* with them.

Master the Science of Miracles® exists to show you the way forward.

But before you can **fully step into this power**, you must first **unlearn the lies you've been told about yourself**.

You have been conditioned to believe that **you are small.**
That you are **separate** from the forces that shape the universe.
That you must **accept** the limits imposed upon you.

But none of that is true.

You are about to remember **who you really are.**

And once you do, nothing will ever be the same.

Section 3 – The Triune Nature of the Human Being

You are not one person.

You are **three**—a triune being, existing in multiple dimensions at once.

This idea is not new. Across cultures, spiritual traditions, and even modern psychology, variations of this concept appear. Some call it **body, mind, and spirit**. Others name it **conscious, subconscious, and superconscious**. In Christianity, it echoes in the Trinity. In Hinduism, it appears in the three aspects of Brahman.

In the Hawaiian tradition of **Huna**, the ancient shamans described this reality with remarkable clarity. They understood that within each of us exist **three distinct selves**, each with its own role, intelligence, and way of perceiving the world.

The Three Selves of the Human Being

◈ **The Subconscious Self (aka Subconscious Mind)** – The keeper of memories, emotions, and instincts. This part of you stores everything you've ever seen, heard, or experienced. It controls your automatic responses—your fears, desires, habits, and deeply ingrained beliefs.

◈ **The Conscious Self (aka Conscious Mind)** – The rational thinker, the decision-maker. This is the part of you that **plans, analyzes, and takes action**. It sets goals, makes choices, and engages with the world through logic and reason.

◈ **Transcendent Self (aka the High Self)** – The eternal, guiding intelligence. It exists beyond the limitations of time and space, overseeing your life with wisdom, love, and power. This is the part of you that **sees the bigger picture, orchestrates synchronicities, and holds the blueprint of your highest potential**.

These three selves **must work together** if you want to create miracles.

But here's where most people struggle: they only identify with the **Conscious Self**—the rational mind. They believe they are **only their thoughts**, their daily to-do lists, their logical reasoning.

They try to manifest their desires by **thinking harder**, **wishing more**, or **forcing** their way through obstacles.

And yet... nothing changes.

The Secret to Unlocking True Power

The ancient Huna masters knew something that modern self-help gurus often miss:

The Conscious Self cannot communicate directly with the Transcendent Self.

No matter how much you **consciously desire** something, your Transcendent Self will only respond if the message is **sent through the Subconscious Self.**

This is why so many people struggle with manifestation.

They create vision boards. They repeat affirmations. They tell themselves, *"I am successful. I am wealthy. I am happy."*

But their **subconscious self** doesn't believe it.

And if the subconscious self doesn't believe it, it **won't send the request to the Transcendent Self**.

Think of it like a divine telephone system. The Transcendent Self is waiting to receive your instructions, ready to bring you **insight, synchronicity, and transformation**.

But the only way to **make the call** is through the Low Self.

And if the subconscious Self is filled with **fear, doubt, or unresolved emotional wounds**, the signal gets **blocked**.

Mastering the Three Selves

The key to working with **Master the Science of Miracles®** is learning how to:

✅ **Build a trusting relationship with the subconscious self** so it willingly delivers your requests to the High Self.

✅ **Clear subconscious resistance** so the subconscious self isn't sabotaging your efforts.

✅ **Charge up vital life energy** so your request has the power to reach the Transcendent Self and manifest in physical reality.

When these three selves work **in harmony**, something extraordinary happens.

Your subconscious stops resisting. Your conscious mind stays **clear and focused**. Your Transcendent Self begins orchestrating events, bringing you insights, synchronicities, and results **faster than you ever thought possible**.

This is **not just a theory**—it's a time-tested process that **has been used for centuries** by those who understood how reality truly works.

But before you can fully engage with this system, there's one essential step: **you must build a relationship with your Low Self.**

Without that, the rest of the process will never work.

So, let's begin.

Section 4 – Preparing for the MSM Process

Now that you understand the **three-part nature of your being**, you might be wondering:

"How do I get my subconscious self, conscious self, and Transcendent Self to work together?"

This is where most people get stuck. They read about manifestation, they try visualization exercises, and they set intentions—but they **don't see results**.

Why?

Because their **subconscious self isn't cooperating**.

The subconscious self is like a **guardian at the gate**—it determines what information gets passed up to the Transcendent Self. If the subconscious self **doubts, fears, or resists your desires**, your message never reaches the Transcendent Self.

This is why **most people struggle with manifestation**. They are trying to create change **consciously**, but their subconscious self is running old programs, unresolved emotions, and limiting beliefs in the background.

So before you can fully engage with **Master the Science of Miracles®**, you must first **prepare the subconscious self** to become a willing partner in the process.

The Three Steps to Preparation
To activate the MSM process, you must:

- ☑ **Build a relationship with your subconscious self**
- ☑ **Train your subconscious self in non-physical perception**
- ☑ **Develop an excess charge of vital life energy**

Each of these steps ensures that your subconscious self is ready to **receive, transmit, and amplify your requests to the Transcendent Self**.

Step 1: Build a Relationship with Your Subconscious Self
Think of your subconscious self as a **separate being living inside you**—a powerful, intelligent entity with its own needs, emotions, and ways of communicating.

Most people ignore or even **battle** with their subconscious self, treating it like a problem to be fixed. But in reality, the subconscious self desperately **wants to help you**—it just needs to be approached in the right way.

To build a relationship, start by:

- **Speaking to it with kindness**—no more self-criticism or negative self-talk.

- **Listening to your emotions and intuitions**—these are how your subconscious self communicates.

20

- **Creating a safe, trusting environment**—the more your subconscious self feels secure, the more it will cooperate.

When your subconscious self **trusts you**, it will **deliver your messages to the Transcendent Self without resistance**—and that's when miracles start happening.

Step 2: Train Your Subconscious Self in Non-Physical Perception
Your subconscious self has **sensing faculties beyond the physical world**. It can pick up on unseen energies, send and receive messages from the Transcendent Self, and access information that your conscious self **cannot perceive**.

But just like a muscle, these abilities must be **trained**.

In **Master the Science of Miracles®**, you'll engage in exercises to:

◈ **Strengthen intuitive perception**—so you can sense guidance from the Transcendent Self.
◈ **Expand awareness beyond the five senses**—so you can pick up on subtle energetic shifts.
◈ **Refine your ability to project consciousness**—so you can directly interact with the fabric of reality.

Once your subconscious self becomes skilled in these practices, it will **naturally connect with the Transcendent Self**, making the MSM process far more effective.

Step 3: Develop an Excess Charge of Vital Life Energy
Most people are **low on energy**—not just physically, but energetically. They go through life exhausted, stressed, and drained, leaving **nothing extra to power their manifestations**.

But manifestation requires **fuel**.

In MSM, **vital life energy** is what **carries** your thought-forms from the subconscious self to the Transcendent Self. Without enough energy, even the most beautifully constructed thought-forms will **fail to take hold in reality**.

That's why **energy cultivation is a non-negotiable step in this process**.

In upcoming chapters, you'll learn how to:

🔥 **Charge up your body's energy reserves** using breathwork and focus techniques.
🔥 **Build a surplus of energy** that can be directed toward manifestation.
🔥 **Use high-energy emotions** (like gratitude and joy) to amplify your desired outcomes.

When your subconscious self is charged with **excess energy**, it becomes far more effective at **delivering requests to the Transcendent Self**—which, in turn, manifests results **faster and with greater clarity**.

Setting the Foundation for Miracles

These three steps—**building trust with your subconscious self, training non-physical perception, and cultivating energy**—are the **foundation** of the MSM process.

Most people fail at manifestation because they **skip these steps**. They focus on **positive thinking** without preparing their subconscious self to actually receive and deliver their requests.

But now, you have a different path.

By laying the groundwork before you begin the full MSM process, you make success far more attainable and the journey much smoother. You are now ready to move forward.

In the next section, we'll explore the **step-by-step process of Master the Science of Miracles®**—and how to **turn thoughts into reality with precision and power**.

Section 5 – The Step-by-Step Process of Master the Science of Miracles®

Now that you understand the **three-part nature of your being** and have laid the groundwork for success, you're ready to step into the actual process of **Master the Science of Miracles®** (MSM).

This is where theory becomes action.

The MSM process is not about **blind belief** or **wishful thinking**—it is a structured, repeatable system that engages the **subconscious self, conscious self, and Transcendent Self** in a way that allows you to create real, measurable results.

Each step builds upon the last, forming a complete cycle that **bridges thought and reality**.

Step 1: Atone for Past Affronts or Injuries to Others

Before you can send a request to the **Transcendent Self**, your **subconscious self must be clear of resistance**. If you have caused harm to others—whether intentionally or unintentionally—this can create **energetic blocks** that interfere with the MSM process.

The subconscious self must **believe that balance has been restored** before it will fully engage.

If possible, atonement should be made directly to the person affected. But if that's not an option, you can use **symbolic actions** to restore balance:

- Acts of **service or charitable giving** with the intention of offsetting past harm.

- Using **the Personal Demon Demolisher** (covered in Chapter 7) to clear guilt and subconscious resistance.

This step is not about **punishment**—it's about **restoring harmony** so that your subconscious self is fully aligned with your desires.

Step 2: Define Your Desired Reality
Many people know exactly what they **don't** want, but struggle to clearly define what they **do** want.

The subconscious self cannot work with vague intentions—it needs a **specific, multi-sensory thought-form** to deliver to the Transcendent Self.

To define your desired reality:

✅ **Be precise.** Instead of saying, *"I want financial freedom,"* describe **exactly** what that looks like. How much money do you have? How do you feel? What kind of lifestyle are you living?

✅ **Engage all senses.** See, hear, feel, smell, and even taste your new reality. The more vivid your thought-form, the more powerful it becomes.

✅ **Infuse it with emotion.** Thought alone is not enough—high-energy emotions like **gratitude, joy, and excitement** give it power.

If resistance arises, it may indicate subconscious blocks. In Chapter 7, you'll learn techniques like **pendulum work and energy clearing** to remove these barriers.

Step 3: Build a Daily MSM Practice
Manifestation isn't a one-time event—it's a **practice**.

Each day, you will engage in a structured process to **charge your thought-form with energy and send it to the Transcendent Self.**

Your daily MSM practice will include:

1 **Charging your energy reserves** through breathwork and focus techniques.
2 **Entering the Alpha state**, where your mind is relaxed and receptive.
3 **Connecting with the Transcendent Self**, affirming your trust in its guidance.
4 **Experiencing your multi-sensory thought-form as present reality.**
5 **Sending the thought-form with excess energy**, ensuring it reaches the Transcendent Self.
6**Ending with gratitude and detachment,** trusting that the process is in motion.

This practice ensures that your subconscious self is **consistently aligned with your vision** and that your Transcendent Self has received the message **with clarity and power**.

Step 4: Stay Focused and Consistent

One of the biggest reasons people fail in manifestation is **scattered focus**. They try to manifest **too many things at once**, or they lose faith if results don't appear immediately.

To stay on track:

✓ **Work on one major intention at a time.** MSM works best when your energy is concentrated.
✓ **Trust the process.** The "how" is not your responsibility—the Transcendent Self orchestrates the details.
✓ **Close each session purposefully.** End with gratitude, not desperation. The more **certainty** you have, the faster the results.

By remaining **focused and consistent**, you allow the MSM process to unfold in its most powerful form.

Stepping Into Mastery

By following these steps, you move from **passive hope** to **active creation**.

You are no longer at the mercy of external circumstances—you are learning to **work with the forces that shape reality** in a deliberate, structured way.

In the next section, we will explore **key principles for success**—the mindsets, habits, and energetic techniques that will **supercharge your ability to manifest with MSM**.

You're no longer just wishing for miracles.

You're learning to **create them.**

Chapter 3: Building Up A Surcharge Of Vital Life-Force Energy

Section 1 – The Mystery of Life Energy

There is a hidden force that powers every living thing—a force that ancient traditions have recognized for thousands of years and that modern science is only beginning to understand.

This force is the **energy of miracles**.

It is the current that runs through every atom, the unseen fabric that connects all things. It flows through the body, the earth, and the cosmos. It is the **spark that turns thought into reality, the fuel that powers transformation, and the bridge between the physical world and the unseen realms**.

Albert Einstein once said, *"The most beautiful thing we can experience is the mysterious. It is the source of all true art and science."*

To master miracles, you must become comfortable with the **mysterious**—not in a way that demands blind belief, but in a way that opens you to **a deeper understanding of the forces that shape reality**.

You already interact with this energy every day, even if you're unaware of it. Every breath you take, every emotion you feel, and every thought you hold carries **an energetic signature**. It influences you, your surroundings, and the events that unfold in your life.

But to use this energy deliberately—to harness it as a tool for transformation—you must first understand its nature.

You Contain the Universe Within You

More than a century ago, **Nikola Tesla** declared, *"If you want to find the secrets of the universe, think in terms of energy, frequency, and vibration."*

Long before Tesla, the great mystics and sages of history had already arrived at this truth.

27

Bahá'u'lláh, the nineteenth-century Prisoner and Exile, wrote: *"Dost thou reckon thyself only a puny form when within thee the universe is folded?"*

"

These words hold a profound meaning—one that goes beyond poetry or philosophy. They point to the **divine reality that exists within you**, a reality that modern physics is beginning to verify:

The universe is not **outside** of you. It exists **within** you.

You are made of the same **energy and intelligence** that forms galaxies, ignites stars, and orchestrates the vast unfolding of existence. You are not separate from the universe—you are an **active participant in its creative process**.

When you begin to understand this, you stop thinking of miracles as **extraordinary events** and start seeing them as **the natural outcome of working with universal energy**.

This is why *Master the Science of Miracles®* is not about wishful thinking or hoping that things will go your way. It is about learning how to **work with** the energy of miracles in a precise, structured, and repeatable way.

To do this, you must first understand **what this energy is, how it moves, and how you can cultivate it to fuel your transformation**.

This chapter will take you beyond theory and into **direct experience**, where you will learn how to **generate, store, and direct this energy with purpose**.

Because once you master the energy of miracles, nothing is beyond your reach.

Section 2 – The Miracle of Universal Vital Life Energy

Across the world, from the ancient wisdom of the East to the indigenous traditions of the Americas, one truth remains constant: **everything is energy**.

Though different cultures have given it different names, they have all recognized a **universal life force** that pervades all things—a force that sustains life, heals the body, and serves as the **bridge between thought and reality**.

- In **China**, it is called **Qi**—the invisible energy that flows through the meridians, governing health and vitality.

- In **India**, it is known as **Prana**—the sacred breath that animates all living beings.

- In **Polynesia**, it is referred to as **Mana**—the spiritual power that can be cultivated and directed.

- Among the **Sioux Nation**, it is called **Wakan**—the sacred essence that connects the material and spiritual worlds.

Despite their differences in language and culture, these traditions all point to the **same fundamental truth**: life is not sustained by physical matter alone. It is fueled by an **invisible, intelligent energy**—an energy that not only exists **within** us but can be cultivated, expanded, and directed.

Ancient Wisdom Meets Modern Science

For centuries, Western science largely ignored the idea of a universal life force. The focus remained on **what could be measured and quantified**, dismissing the unseen as superstition.

But over time, discoveries in **quantum physics, bioenergetics, and consciousness research** have begun to validate what ancient traditions have known all along.

Physicists now acknowledge that at the most fundamental level, everything in the universe is **made of vibrating energy fields**. Matter is not solid—it is energy held in patterns by invisible forces.

In groundbreaking studies, researchers have observed that **human intention** can influence matter, energy fields, and even biological systems. Scientists at institutions like the **HeartMath Institute** have demonstrated that the **human heart emits an electromagnetic field that can extend several feet beyond the body**—and that this field is directly influenced by emotions and intention.

What this means is profound:

You are not just a physical being. You are an energetic being, constantly sending and receiving information in ways that go beyond the five senses.

And once you begin to **work with** this energy—rather than being controlled by it—you unlock the potential for **miracles to unfold in your life with precision and clarity**.

The Foundation of the MSM Process
In *Master the Science of Miracles®*, vital life energy is the **foundation** of everything you will learn.

It is the **fuel** that powers the MSM process.

Without an excess charge of energy, even the most carefully constructed thought-forms **lack the power to reach the Transcendent Self**. The process becomes slow, inconsistent, or ineffective—not because the principles are flawed, but because the energy behind them is too weak.

This is why energy cultivation is **not optional** in MSM.

It is a **required skill**—one that must be **developed, strengthened, and mastered**.

In the next sections, you will learn how to:
✓ **Generate** vital life energy through specific breathing and focus

techniques.

✓ **Store** this energy in the **Lower Dan Tian**, the body's natural energy reservoir.

✓ **Direct** this energy toward your thought-forms, ensuring they reach the Transcendent Self with maximum power.

These are not abstract concepts. They are **practical, repeatable techniques** that have been used for centuries by those who understood how reality truly works.

Once you learn to cultivate and control the **energy of miracles**, your ability to manifest will no longer be left to chance.

It will become a **deliberate, structured process—one that works with the same certainty as the certainty of the sun rising in the east.**

Section 3 – Cultivating and Developing Your Vital Life Energy

Understanding the **energy of miracles** is one thing. **Harnessing** it is another.

To make the *Master the Science of Miracles®* process work for you, your subconscious self must have **an excess charge of vital life energy**. Without it, even the most vivid thought-forms will struggle to reach the Transcendent Self.

This is where most people fail in manifestation—they rely on **thought alone**, not realizing that **energy is the vehicle that carries thought into reality**.

The subconscious self has **three primary responsibilities** when it comes to vital life energy:

1 **Maintaining the body's autonomic functions**—regulating the heartbeat, digestion, breathing, and immune response.

2 **Providing energy for conscious activities**—fueling decision-making, creativity, problem-solving, and physical movement.

3 **Transmitting thought-forms to the Transcendent Self**—converting desires into **energetic blueprints** that can be realized in physical form.

Most people unknowingly **exhaust their energy** on the first two functions, leaving very little available for the third.

Why Most People Operate with Low Energy

In today's world, most people are running on **low energy reserves** without realizing it.

They wake up tired. They rely on caffeine or sugar to push through the day. They feel mentally foggy, emotionally drained, and physically exhausted—sometimes despite getting enough sleep.

This is because they are constantly **leaking energy** through:

✗ **Negative emotions**—worry, fear, resentment, and self-doubt drain life force.
✗ **Overthinking and indecision**—excessive mental activity burns energy without results.
✗ **Lack of breath awareness**—most people breathe **shallowly**, starving the body of vital energy.
✗ **Poor energetic hygiene**—unconsciously absorbing the stress and emotions of others.

When the body is **low on energy**, it prioritizes **physical survival** over anything else.

This means the subconscious self has **little to no energy left** to send thought-forms to the Transcendent Self, making manifestation slow, weak, or completely ineffective.

This is why **energy cultivation is not optional in MSM**—it is a **required foundation** for everything else to work.

Building a Surplus of Energy
To manifest effectively, you must learn how to **generate, store, and direct** vital life energy with intention.

This begins with:

✓ **Daily energy cultivation practices**—breathing, focus, and movement techniques that build energy reserves.
✓ **Training the subconscious self to hold an excess charge**—ensuring enough energy is available for manifestation.
✓ **Minimizing energy leaks**—clearing subconscious blocks and emotional patterns that drain energy.

Once your subconscious self consistently holds **a surplus of energy**, your ability to manifest becomes **exponentially stronger**.

In the next section, we will explore **how the subconscious self manages energy** and why learning to control it is the key to unlocking your full potential.

Section 4 – The Role of the Subconscious Self in Energy Management
The subconscious self is the **gatekeeper of your energy**.

It is responsible for **gathering, storing, and distributing vital life energy**—deciding where energy is allocated, how much is used, and when it is conserved. Without its cooperation, no amount of effort from your conscious self will be enough to create real change.

If you've ever set an intention but felt drained, distracted, or unable to follow through, **your subconscious self was not supplying enough energy to the process**.

This is why cultivating **a surplus charge of energy** is one of the most important steps in *Master the Science of Miracles*®. Without enough energy, even the most well-formed thought-forms **fail to reach the Transcendent Self**.

The Subconscious Self's Energy Priorities

The subconscious self has **a strict hierarchy** when it comes to energy distribution. It will always prioritize:

1 **Survival and bodily functions** – Breathing, digestion, heart rate, immune function.
2 **Daily conscious activities** – Decision-making, emotions, movement, and mental processing.
3 **Transmitting thought-forms to the Transcendent Self** – Sending multi-sensory thought-forms upward to be realized in physical form.

If your energy levels are **low**, the subconscious self will devote everything to **the first two functions**, leaving little to no energy for **manifestation, intuitive perception, or high-level thinking**.

This is why many people feel:
✗ **Drained or unfocused when trying to visualize their desires**
✗ **Emotionally blocked when attempting to change their reality**
✗ **Disconnected from the guidance of their Transcendent Self**

Their subconscious self is simply **conserving energy for survival**— not because it's resisting their desires, but because **there isn't enough energy to spare**.

The key to unlocking **high-level manifestation** is to **reverse this energy scarcity** by training the subconscious self to:

☑ **Generate and hold excess energy** rather than running on depletion.
☑ **Prioritize thought-form transmission** alongside bodily functions.
☑ **Send a clear, high-energy message to the Transcendent Self** without interference.

When this happens, manifestation becomes **natural and effortless**, because your subconscious self is no longer working against you—it is **powering the process**.

How the Subconscious Self Controls Energy Flow

The subconscious self does not think in words—it operates through **patterns, emotions, and physical sensations**.

This means that if you want to direct your energy **deliberately**, you must **train the subconscious self** to recognize and hold higher energy levels.

There are three key ways to do this:

1 **Breathwork and Energy Cultivation** – Learning to consciously charge the body with life energy.
2 **Lower Dan Tian Awareness** – Storing and managing energy in the body's primary reservoir.
3 **Energetic Projection** – Directing vital life energy outward for manifestation.

In the next section, we will begin with the **foundation of all energy work—breath**.

Because before you can **command** your energy, you must first **generate it**.

Section 5 – Breathing: The Foundation of Energy Cultivation

Breath is the **first and most fundamental** way to generate vital life energy.

From the moment you take your first breath at birth to your last breath in this lifetime, **your body depends on the rhythmic exchange of air to sustain life**. But breathing does far more than just provide oxygen—it is the primary method for cultivating and directing the **energy of miracles**.

Every mystical tradition that has worked with life energy—whether Qi, Prana, Mana, or Wakan—has recognized that **breath is the key to harnessing and controlling it**.

But here's the problem: **most people breathe incorrectly.**

They take shallow, unconscious breaths that only fill the upper lungs, starving the body of energy. This kind of breathing keeps the nervous system in **a state of stress, tension, and depletion**—forcing the subconscious self to **prioritize survival over manifestation**.

To reverse this, you must learn how to **breathe properly**, using techniques that allow your body to **generate, store, and circulate vital life energy**.

Why Breath is the Key to Energy Control

Your subconscious self regulates **all automatic bodily functions**, but breath is unique because it is the **only autonomic function that can be consciously controlled**.

This means that by **changing the way you breathe**, you can directly influence:

✅ **Your energy levels** – generating a steady supply of vital life energy.
✅ **Your mental and emotional state** – shifting from stress to calm, from scattered to focused.
✅ **Your subconscious programming** – training it to hold and direct energy for manifestation.

By practicing **conscious breathing techniques**, you communicate to your subconscious self:

"I am in control of my energy. I am generating an excess charge. I am ready to direct this energy toward my desired reality."

The Problems with Modern Breathing Habits

Most people breathe in a way that is:

✗ **Too shallow** – only using the upper chest instead of the full lungs.
✗ **Too fast** – keeping the body in a constant state of mild panic.
✗ **Too unconscious** – disconnected from awareness, running on autopilot.

These habits **weaken the energy system**, preventing the subconscious self from accumulating and transmitting the **power needed for manifestation**.

To **reverse this**, you must retrain yourself to breathe **deeply, slowly, and deliberately**—activating your body's natural ability to generate and store life energy.

The Foundation of Energy Cultivation: Deep Belly Breathing
The most effective way to begin cultivating vital life energy is through **deep belly breathing**—also known as **diaphragmatic breathing**.

This method has been used in:

◈ **Ancient Chinese Qi cultivation** to build and circulate Qi.
◈ **Yogic traditions in India** to enhance Prana and awaken spiritual potential.
◈ **Modern breathwork practices** to reduce stress and amplify energy levels.

How to Practice Deep Belly Breathing

1 **Sit or stand in a relaxed position.** Keep your spine naturally straight, allowing for full breath expansion.

2 **Place one hand on your chest and the other on your lower abdomen.**

3 **Inhale slowly through your nose, expanding your belly first, then your ribs, then your upper chest.**

- Imagine the air filling your **Lower Dan Tian**, just below your navel.

- Feel your **abdomen expand outward** as you breathe in.

4 Exhale slowly through your mouth, gently drawing your belly inward.

- Imagine releasing any **stagnant energy** or tension.

- Allow the breath to leave in a smooth, controlled flow.

5 Repeat for 5–10 minutes.

- With each breath, feel your **body becoming charged with vital life energy**.

- If your mind wanders, bring your focus back to the sensation of your breath.

The First Step in Energy Mastery

Breath is your **direct connection** to the energy of miracles.

By practicing **deep belly breathing daily**, you are:

☑ **Training your subconscious self to generate and hold more energy.**
☑ **Preparing your system to store and direct that energy effectively.**
☑ **Strengthening your ability to send high-energy thought-forms to the Transcendent Self.**

This is just the beginning.

In the next section, you will learn about the **Lower Dan Tian—the body's natural energy reservoir—**and how to use it to **store and amplify the life energy you generate through breathwork**.

The deeper your mastery of breath, the stronger your connection to **the energy of miracles**.

Section 6 – Locating Your Lower Dan Tian: The Body's Energy Reservoir

Breath is the **first step** in generating the energy of miracles. But to truly harness this energy, you must learn how to **store it** effectively.

Just as a **battery holds power for later use**, your body has a **natural energy reservoir**—a place where **vital life energy is collected, refined, and distributed** throughout your system.

This reservoir is called the **Lower Dan Tian**.

For thousands of years, Eastern energy masters have described the **Lower Dan Tian as the foundation of internal power**—the **core of physical, mental, and spiritual energy storage**. Whether in Chinese Qi cultivation, Indian Pranayama practices, or martial arts training, **all high-level energy work begins with developing the Lower Dan Tian**.

What is the Lower Dan Tian?
The Lower Dan Tian is your body's **primary energy storage center**. It is where the **energy you generate through breathwork, movement, and focus is stored and refined** before being directed toward higher-level practices, such as:

✓ **Strengthening the body's energy field.**
✓ **Amplifying mental clarity and emotional stability.**
✓ **Fueling the transmission of thought-forms to the Transcendent Self.**

Think of it as the **power generator of your being**—the stronger it becomes, the more energy you have available for **manifestation, healing, and spiritual connection**.

How to Locate Your Lower Dan Tian
1 **Sit or stand in a relaxed position.** Keep your spine naturally straight, allowing for full energy flow.

2 **Place one hand on your navel.** Now move your hand about three finger-widths **below** your belly button.

3 **Imagine a point deep within your abdomen, about halfway between your navel and your spine.** This is your **Lower Dan Tian—** your **energy center**.

4 **Breathe deeply into this area.** As you inhale, feel your belly expand outward, as if you are drawing energy into this central point.

5 **As you exhale, gently contract your lower abdomen, guiding the energy deeper into the Lower Dan Tian.**

At first, you may not feel anything unusual. But with practice, this area will become **warm, tingly, or even slightly pressurized**—a sign that your energy is building.

Why Strengthening the Lower Dan Tian is Essential

If your **Lower Dan Tian is weak**, your ability to:
X **Hold energy for extended periods** is limited.
X **Direct energy toward manifestation** becomes inconsistent.
X **Maintain mental and emotional stability** is difficult.

When you strengthen the Lower Dan Tian, however:
☑ **Your subconscious self learns to store an excess charge of energy.**
☑ **Your ability to send high-energy thought-forms to the Transcendent Self increases.**
☑ **Your mind becomes clearer, emotions more balanced, and manifestations more precise.**

This is why **energy cultivation starts here**. Without a **charged Lower Dan Tian**, the subconscious self has **nothing to send upward**—no fuel for thought-forms, no power for transformation.

Activating the Lower Dan Tian for Manifestation

Once your Lower Dan Tian is activated and **regularly charged with energy**, you can use it to:

🜄 **Strengthen and stabilize your personal energy field.**
🜄 **Amplify high-vibration emotions like gratitude, joy, and love.**
🜄 **Project energy outward into your thought-forms, giving them greater power.**

In the next section, we will explore **specific exercises** that will allow you to **store and control this energy** with precision—ensuring that every intention you send is infused with the power of the **energy of miracles**.

Section 7 – The Seated Exercise: Breathing to Cultivate Energy

Now that you've located your **Lower Dan Tian**, the next step is to begin **filling it with energy**.

This is done through a simple yet powerful practice: **seated breathing for energy cultivation**.

This exercise trains your **subconscious self** to:
☑ **Draw in and accumulate vital life energy.**
☑ **Strengthen the Lower Dan Tian as a stable energy reservoir.**
☑ **Prepare for the advanced energy work required for manifestation.**

By practicing daily, you **condition your subconscious self** to store and circulate energy effortlessly—building the foundation for working with the **energy of miracles**.

The Seated Energy Cultivation Exercise
1 **Find a Quiet, Comfortable Place**

- Sit in a **comfortable but upright** position—either on a chair with both feet on the floor or cross-legged on a cushion.

- Keep your **spine naturally straight** to allow for unrestricted energy flow.

2 Relax the Body

- Let your shoulders, face, and jaw soften—**release any unnecessary tension**.

- Close your eyes if it helps you focus inward.

3 Focus on Your Breath

- Place one hand lightly on your Lower Dan Tian (three finger-widths below your navel).

- Breathe in slowly through your **nose**, directing the breath deep into your lower abdomen.

- Feel your belly gently **expand outward** as you inhale.

- Exhale **slowly and fully** through your mouth, drawing your belly inward.

- Maintain a **smooth, unforced rhythm**—your breath should be deep, but natural.

4 Engage the Mind

- As you breathe in, imagine **golden light** flowing into your Lower Dan Tian.

- As you exhale, visualize this energy **settling and condensing**, becoming stronger with each breath.

- Feel a sense of warmth or slight tingling as the energy builds.

5 Continue for 5–10 Minutes

- With each cycle, your Lower Dan Tian **stores more energy**.

- You may begin to feel a slight **heaviness, warmth, or tingling** in your lower abdomen—this is a sign that your subconscious self is responding.

The Benefits of This Practice

By practicing **daily**, you will:

✓ **Train your subconscious self to store and hold an excess charge of energy.**

✓ **Develop greater stability in your personal energy field.**

✓ **Strengthen your ability to send energy-powered thought-forms to the Transcendent Self.**

Many people notice **increased mental clarity, emotional balance, and even physical vitality** after just a few weeks of practice.

Over time, your subconscious self will **automatically maintain a higher energy level**—allowing you to operate from a place of abundance rather than depletion.

In the next section, we will explore a **standing energy exercise**—one that builds upon this practice by allowing you to **generate, store, and control even greater amounts of vital life energy**.

Section 8 – The Standing Exercise: Generating and Controlling Energy

Now that you've learned how to **store energy in the Lower Dan Tian** using seated breathing, the next step is to **generate and control even greater amounts of energy** through **standing practice**.

This exercise trains your **subconscious self** to:

- ☑ **Expand your ability to generate vital life energy.**
- ☑ **Strengthen your connection to your body's energy field.**
- ☑ **Increase your control over energy movement and projection.**

It builds upon the **seated practice** by introducing a **dynamic posture** that **activates energy flow, deepens awareness, and strengthens your energetic foundation**.

The Standing Energy Cultivation Exercise
1 Find a Quiet Space and Stand in a Relaxed Position

- Stand with your feet **shoulder-width apart**, knees slightly bent.

- Keep your **spine naturally aligned**, not rigid.

- Let your shoulders, arms, and jaw relax.

2 Set Your Energy Posture

- **Gently tilt your pelvis forward** so your weight is balanced.

- **Relax your chest** and let your arms hang naturally at your sides.

- Keep your **head lifted** as if suspended by an invisible thread from the crown.

3 Hold the Energy Ball Position

- Slowly **raise your arms in front of you**, as if cradling a **large, invisible ball of energy**.

- Your hands should be about **chest level**, with elbows slightly bent and fingers relaxed.

- Imagine this space between your hands **filling with energy**—a glowing sphere that grows stronger with each breath.

4 Breathe into Your Lower Dan Tian

- Inhale deeply through your nose, feeling the breath sink **into your lower abdomen**.

- As you exhale through your mouth, imagine the energy **settling and condensing** in the Lower Dan Tian.

- Maintain a **smooth, relaxed breathing pattern**, allowing energy to circulate naturally.

5 Feel the Energy Begin to Move

- As you continue to breathe, you may feel:

    - A gentle **tingling or warmth** in your hands.

    - A **magnetic sensation** between your palms.

    - A sense that your arms are being **subtly lifted by energy**, rather than muscle effort.

6 Hold the Posture for 5–10 Minutes

- Remain still, allowing the energy to **build and circulate**.

- If your arms become tired, relax them briefly, then return to the position.

The Purpose of the Standing Practice
This exercise is designed to:
✓ **Increase your ability to generate and hold energy.**
✓ **Train your subconscious self to direct energy at will.**
✓ **Enhance your sensitivity to energy movement and flow.**

While the **seated exercise** focuses on **accumulating energy**, the **standing exercise** allows you to:
🔥 **Feel the tangible presence of energy within and around you.**
🔥 **Develop control over how energy moves through your system.**
🔥 **Prepare for higher-level practices, such as projecting energy into your thought-forms.**

When to Practice

For best results, alternate between **seated and standing practice** daily:

- **Morning:** Standing practice to **activate and circulate energy**.

- **Evening:** Seated practice to **store and consolidate energy**.

By practicing consistently, you will:

☑ **Train your subconscious self to work with energy automatically.**

☑ **Develop a strong energy foundation for manifestation.**

☑ **Increase the power of your thought-forms, making them more effective.**

In the next section, we will explore how to **project energy outward**—allowing you to use this cultivated life force to influence the world around you.

Section 9 – Projecting Your Energy Outward

Now that you've learned how to **generate and store vital life energy**, the next step is to **project that energy outward**.

This is where your cultivated energy becomes **a tool for transformation**.

Your subconscious self now holds an **excess charge** of energy, and instead of letting it remain contained, you will learn how to **release and direct it with intention**—whether for healing, manifestation, or strengthening your connection to the Transcendent Self.

This is the **next stage of working with the energy of miracles**—moving from **internal cultivation to external influence**.

The Principle of Energy Projection

Energy flows like **water**.

Wherever you **direct your attention**, your energy follows—just like a stream of water **flowing downhill**.

This is why:
✓ **Your emotions influence those around you.**
✓ **Your thoughts can be sensed by others before you speak them.**
✓ **Some people seem to radiate presence and confidence without saying a word.**

When your subconscious self **learns to direct energy intentionally**, you gain the ability to:
🐉 **Charge your multi-sensory thought-forms with power.**
🐉 **Influence your environment energetically.**
🐉 **Strengthen your connection with people, places, and even events.**

This ability is not **imaginary or mystical**—it is a **trainable skill**, just like developing a muscle.

The Energy Projection Exercise
Now, you will practice **projecting energy from your Lower Dan Tian, through your arms, and out through your hands**—just like **water flowing through a hose**.

1 **Begin in a Seated or Standing Position**

- Choose the position that feels most natural to you—**seated for stillness, standing for greater energy flow**.

- **Relax your entire body**, allowing your energy to settle.

2 **Activate Your Lower Dan Tian**

- Place your focus on your **Lower Dan Tian**, just below your navel.

- Breathe deeply, feeling the breath sink into this area.

- Imagine **water pooling in your Lower Dan Tian**, like a **well filling with fresh, flowing water**.

3 Draw Energy Upward

- As you inhale, **imagine drawing water up from the Lower Dan Tian**—like pulling water from a deep well.

- As you exhale, **let the water flow down your arms** toward your hands.

- Feel this **cool, refreshing stream** begin to circulate through your body.

4 Project the Energy

- Extend your hands outward, palms facing forward or slightly cupped.

- Imagine **a stream of water flowing out from your palms**, like a gentle river pouring into the space in front of you.

- This energy can be directed toward:
  ◊ **A person** (for healing or strengthening connection).
  ◊ **An object** (to charge it with intention).
  ◊ **A thought-form** (to give it power before sending it to the Transcendent Self).

5 Feel the Feedback

- Pay attention to **sensations in your hands**—a coolness, a slight heaviness, or the **subtle flow of energy like water trickling down your fingers**.

- If your hands feel **full or weighty**, you are successfully projecting energy.

- If you feel nothing at first, continue practicing—**awareness develops with time**.

6 Release and Recharge

- After a few minutes, **lower your hands** and place them on your Lower Dan Tian.

- Breathe deeply, feeling the energy **returning like water flowing back into a reservoir**.

- End with a sense of **calm and completion**.

The Purpose of Energy Projection

By learning to project energy outward, you gain the ability to:

✓ **Charge your multi-sensory thought-forms before sending them to the Transcendent Self.**
✓ **Strengthen energetic connections with people, objects, and environments.**
✓ **Influence the world around you in a tangible, measurable way.**

This practice **prepares you for the advanced manifestation work ahead**, ensuring that **your energy is strong enough to create real change**.

In the next section, we will explore how **energy moves beyond time and space**—and why the energy of miracles is not bound by physical limitations.

Section 10 – Expanding Awareness: How Energy Moves Beyond Space and Time

By now, you've learned how to **generate, store, and project vital life energy**. But there's one more crucial insight to understand:

Energy is not bound by space and time.

While physical matter is constrained by distance and location, **energy and intention are not**.

You've likely experienced this yourself:

◈ Thinking of someone moments before they call or text you.
◈ Feeling a strong emotional shift when entering a room where an argument just took place.
◈ Sensing someone's presence before you physically see them.

These experiences happen because **energy moves instantly**, regardless of distance.

When you send energy—whether through thought, intention, or direct projection—it does **not** travel like a physical object. Instead, it is **instantaneously received** by whatever it is directed toward.

This is why the **energy of miracles works beyond logic**—it follows the laws of **consciousness, not physics**.

Scientific and Mystical Insights on Non-Local Energy
Modern science has begun to verify what ancient mystics already knew:

1 **Quantum Entanglement** – Experiments show that when two particles become "entangled," a change in one is instantly reflected in the other, even if they are **light-years apart**.

2 **Remote Healing Studies** – Research has demonstrated that energy healing can **affect people across vast distances**, even when they are unaware it's happening.

3 **The Global Consciousness Project** – Data from this decades-long study suggests that **human consciousness can influence physical systems on a worldwide scale**.

These findings align with what spiritual traditions have always taught:

- The **universe is interconnected**—nothing is truly separate.

- Consciousness **transcends time and space**—your thoughts and emotions extend far beyond your physical body.

- Energy follows **intention**—where you focus, your energy flows.

This means that when you project **vital life energy** to a person, object, or thought-form, **it arrives instantly**.

How This Applies to the MSM Process
The realization that **energy is non-local** changes how you approach *Master the Science of Miracles®*:

✓ **Your multi-sensory thought-forms do not "travel" to the Transcendent Self—they are received the moment they are fully formed.**
✓ **You don't have to "send" energy to people or situations—you simply focus, and the energy connects instantly.**
✓ **Your influence extends beyond what you can see—you are already affecting the future before it unfolds.**

This is why MSM works **even when logical reasoning says it shouldn't**.

It doesn't rely on physical effort alone—it works at the **level of energy and consciousness**, which operate beyond the limits of time and space.

Experiencing Non-Local Energy for Yourself
To fully grasp this concept, it's important to **experience it firsthand**.

Try this simple exercise:

1 **Think of a loved one who is not physically near you.**
2 **Close your eyes and picture them clearly in your mind.**
3 **Imagine gently sending a stream of energy to them, like a flowing current of water.**
4 **Feel a sense of warmth or connection as the energy reaches them.**

5 **Within the next few hours or days, notice if they unexpectedly reach out to you.**

Many people report that after doing this exercise, the person they thought of will:
📞 **Call or text them unexpectedly.**
💡 **Mention that they were "just thinking" about them.**
🌊 **Describe feeling a sudden wave of peace, warmth, or love at the time the energy was sent.**

This is **not coincidence**—this is how energy moves.

By practicing this awareness, you begin to **see the world differently**—not as a collection of separate objects, but as an interconnected field of energy, thought, and intention.

A New Perspective on Reality

Once you understand that **energy transcends space and time**, you stop seeing *Master the Science of Miracles®* as just a process.

It becomes a **way of interacting with reality itself**.

✓ **You realize that your thoughts are not confined to your mind— they influence the world around you.**
✓ **You stop feeling "stuck" in situations, knowing you can shift them through energy and intention.**
✓ **You begin to trust in the unseen connections that shape your life.**

And this is where the **real magic happens**.

In the next chapter, we will explore **how the mind interacts with energy**—specifically, how different brainwave states influence your ability to receive guidance, accelerate manifestation, and create powerful multi-sensory thought-forms.

Because once you understand how **your consciousness shapes energy**, you will unlock the full potential of the energy of miracles.

Final Thoughts on Energy and Space-Time

💡 **Energy moves instantly, without needing time to "travel."**

💡 **Your thoughts and intentions have a real, measurable impact.**

💡 **MSM operates beyond physical limitations, working at the level of consciousness.**

As you move forward, remember: **you are never separate from the energy of the universe.**

You are always connected.

And when you master that connection, miracles become a natural part of your life.

Section 11 – Preparing for the Next Level

At this point, you've learned how to **generate, store, project, and direct** the energy of miracles. You now understand that **energy moves instantly**, transcending the limitations of space and time.

But knowledge alone isn't enough.

To fully integrate these principles into your life, you must **train yourself to work with energy effortlessly**—to move from thinking about energy to **living in harmony with it**.

This is where *Master the Science of Miracles*® becomes more than just a system—it becomes **a way of operating in the world**.

Building the Energy Mindset

Mastering the **energy of miracles** isn't about occasional practice—it's about adopting a mindset that:

✓ **Recognizes energy as the fundamental substance of reality.**
✓ **Understands that thought, intention, and focus influence**

energy.

✓ **Trains the subconscious self to generate, store, and transmit energy with precision.**

By embracing this perspective, you shift from:

✗ **Hoping things will change** → to **deliberately influencing reality.**

✗ **Forcing outcomes through physical effort** → to **aligning with energy flow.**

✗ **Feeling disconnected from miracles** → to **becoming a conduit for them.**

This is **not about control**—it's about **partnership**. You are not bending reality to your will—you are learning how to **work with the unseen forces already at play**.

The more you engage with these practices, the more you will experience **synchronicities, intuitive insights, and effortless manifestations**.

What once seemed like rare miracles will become **a predictable part of your life**.

The Next Step: Mastering the Mind's Role in Manifestation

Energy is only **one half of the equation**.

The other half is **the mind's role in shaping reality**.

Your brain operates in different **wave states**, each influencing:

🧠 **Your ability to access intuitive guidance.**

🧠 **Your subconscious programming.**

🧠 **Your effectiveness in sending thought-forms to the Transcendent Self.**

In the next chapter, we will explore:

✓ **How to enter the Alpha state to bypass resistance.**

✓ **Why multi-sensory thought-forms must be constructed in a specific mental state.**

✓ The relationship between consciousness, energy, and the physical world.

The deeper your understanding, the more effective your MSM practice will become.

Because when you learn to align **your energy, mind, and Transcendent Self**, you step into a reality where miracles are **not just possible—they are inevitable**.

Final Thoughts
You are no longer simply **learning about energy**—you are becoming someone who **lives and breathes the energy of miracles**.

- ✅ You now understand how to **generate, store, and direct energy.**
- ✅ You recognize that **energy moves beyond space and time.**
- ✅ You have begun training your **subconscious self to hold an excess charge.**

With these foundations in place, you are ready for the next level.

In the next chapter, we will explore **the mind's role in manifestation**, unlocking the power of **mental states, thought-forms, and projection techniques**.

Because when you learn to master **both energy and consciousness**, you will become **unstoppable**.

Key Takeaways from Chapter 3
💡 **Energy is the foundation of manifestation—without it, thought-forms lack power.**
💡 **The subconscious self must be trained to store and direct an excess charge of energy.**
💡 **Energy transcends space and time—your intentions are received instantly.**

💡 **Miracles are not random; they are the result of working with energy in a structured way.**

This chapter has laid the groundwork. Now, it's time to take the next step.

The mind **holds the blueprint**.
The energy **fuels the process**.
The Transcendent Self **makes it real**.

Are you ready to master the next level?

Chapter 4: Becoming Acquainted With Your Subconscious Self

Section 1 – Understanding the Subconscious Self

You are not just a single, unified being.

You exist as a **triune self**, composed of **the conscious self, the subconscious self, and the Transcendent Self**. Each part plays a vital role in your life, yet for most people, only one of these—the **conscious self**—gets all the attention.

But the **subconscious self** is the true **powerhouse** behind your experiences.

It is the **bridge** between your **conscious desires and the Transcendent Self's ability to shape reality**. If that bridge is **clear and strong**, your ability to create change in your life is swift and effective. If the bridge is **clogged with emotional debris, limiting beliefs, or untrained energy**, manifestation becomes slow, difficult, or impossible.

To master *Master the Science of Miracles®*, you must first **understand and train the subconscious self**—because it is the **gateway to everything**.

The Three-Part Nature of Human Beings

Throughout history, spiritual traditions and modern psychology alike have recognized the idea that human beings are **more than just a body and mind**.

This is why many belief systems speak of **body, mind, and spirit** or the **conscious, subconscious, and superconscious** aspects of self.

In *Master the Science of Miracles®*, we align with this understanding:

1 **The Conscious Self** – The rational, thinking mind that makes choices, sets goals, and navigates daily life.

2 **The Subconscious Self** – The feeling, sensing, memory-holding self that governs automatic functions, emotions, and energy.
3 **The Transcendent Self** – The highest intelligence within you, connected to the divine, guiding your life's journey.

These three parts are **not separate entities**—they are aspects of the same being, working in different ways. But the **key to transformation** lies in the subconscious self, because it is the **only part of you that can communicate directly with the Transcendent Self**.

Your conscious self **cannot** send thought-forms or intentions directly to the Transcendent Self. Every thought, emotion, and desire must first **pass through the subconscious self**.

This is why your subconscious self **must be trained and refined**—because it is the **channel through which all manifestations occur**.

The Subconscious Self as the Gateway
Rúmí once said:

"Everything in the universe is within you. Ask all from yourself."

This is not just poetic wisdom—it is a **literal truth**.

If you want to unlock the **mysteries of creation**, if you want to **harness the energy of miracles**, you must first turn inward—to the subconscious self.

It is **the record keeper** of everything you have ever experienced.
It is **the energy manager** that distributes vital life force energy throughout your system.
It is **the transmitter** that sends your thought-forms to the Transcendent Self.

And yet, most people go through life completely unaware of it.

They let their subconscious self run on **automatic programming**, shaped by childhood experiences, societal conditioning, and past emotional wounds. They try to change their lives by **thinking harder,**

working harder, or visualizing their goals, without realizing that if their subconscious self **does not accept the goal**, it **will not deliver the request** to the Transcendent Self.

This is why many people struggle with **manifestation and transformation**.

The subconscious self is **the key**, and in this chapter, you will learn **how to work with it rather than against it**.

The Goal of This Chapter
The purpose of this chapter is to help you:

✓ **Understand the subconscious self's role in your life.**
✓ **Learn how it manages energy, emotions, and memory.**
✓ **Recognize its power as the gateway to the Transcendent Self.**
✓ **Begin developing a direct relationship with it.**

Because once you **train the subconscious self**, your ability to manifest miracles becomes **predictable, structured, and repeatable**.

The subconscious self **holds the key to unlocking your full potential**.

Now, let's explore how it actually functions—starting with its **relationship to different brainwave states** and why shifting your mental frequency is the first step in working with it consciously.

Section 2 – Brainwave States and the Subconscious Self
The subconscious self operates in a **different frequency range** than the conscious self.

If you've ever struggled to communicate with your subconscious self—whether through meditation, visualization, or even self-reflection—it's not because the subconscious is unwilling to cooperate. It's because you were trying to reach it **on the wrong frequency**.

Your mind is like a radio receiver.

If you're tuned to the **wrong station**, you get static. But when you adjust to the **right frequency**, you hear the message clearly.

This is why accessing and influencing the subconscious self requires working **at the brainwave frequencies where it naturally operates**.

The Five Brainwave States
Your brain is constantly producing **electrical activity**, which scientists measure in **waves per second** (Hertz). Different mental states correspond to different **brainwave frequencies**, and each plays a unique role in how you experience reality.

◈ **Beta (12-30 Hz) – The Waking Conscious Self**

- Active thinking, problem-solving, and logical reasoning.

- The state you're in when working, planning, or engaged in a conversation.

- **Weakest connection to the subconscious self.**

◈ **Alpha (7.5-12 Hz) – The Gateway to the Subconscious**

- Relaxed, alert, and open to intuition.

- The state between wakefulness and sleep—what you experience during **light meditation, creative flow, or daydreaming**.

- **The ideal state for communicating with the subconscious self.**

◈ **Theta (4-7.5 Hz) – Deep Access to the Subconscious Self**

- The dream state, deep meditation, and heightened suggestibility.

- Where **long-term memories, deep emotions, and subconscious programs reside**.

60

- The most effective state for **rewiring subconscious patterns and embedding thought-forms.**

◈ **Delta (0.5-4 Hz) – The Realm of Deep Healing and Connection**

- The state of **deep, dreamless sleep.**

- Where the subconscious self connects to **the collective unconscious.**

- The state where **physical and emotional healing** is most powerful.

◈ **Gamma (30-100 Hz) – The Superconscious State**

- The frequency of **high-level insights, peak states, and spiritual breakthroughs.**

- Rarely sustained for long periods—flashes of **genius, intuition, or divine inspiration** occur here.

- In MSM, **Gamma bursts are seen as signs of direct interaction with the Transcendent Self.**

Why This Matters for Manifestation

Most people try to influence the subconscious self while in **Beta**—the thinking, logical state.

That's like trying to plant a seed in **hardened, dry soil**. The conscious self is **too active, too critical, too caught up in immediate concerns** to allow deep transformation to take root.

To truly access and **reprogram the subconscious self**, you must enter **Alpha or Theta states**.

✓ **Alpha is where the subconscious becomes receptive.**
✓ **Theta is where subconscious programs are rewritten.**

This is why practices like **meditation, hypnosis, visualization, and deep breathing** are so effective—they lower your brainwave state into the range where the subconscious self operates naturally.

The Ideal Brainwave State for MSM

To communicate with and direct the subconscious self, you need to:

1 **Lower your brainwaves to Alpha or Theta.**

- Relaxation exercises, meditation, and rhythmic breathing help shift from Beta to Alpha.

- Deeper techniques, such as guided visualization and focused attention, bring you into Theta.

2 **Engage the subconscious with vivid multi-sensory thought-forms.**

- The subconscious doesn't respond to logic—it responds to **images, emotions, and sensory experiences**.

- This is why MSM uses **multi-sensory thought-forms** rather than just affirmations or positive thinking.

3 **Charge the thought-form with vital life energy.**

- Thought alone is not enough—the subconscious self needs **an excess charge of energy** to send the request to the Transcendent Self.

- This is why MSM integrates **breathwork and energy cultivation** into the manifestation process.

When you work **with** your subconscious self at the right brainwave frequency, the process becomes **effortless and natural**.

Tuning Your Mind to the Right Frequency

Imagine you are trying to call a friend, but your phone is **set to the wrong country code**.

It doesn't matter how many times you dial—the connection won't go through.

This is what happens when people try to **consciously manifest desires while in Beta**. Their conscious mind is full of **doubt, analysis, and resistance**, blocking the message from ever reaching the subconscious self—let alone the Transcendent Self.

To truly **align with the energy of miracles**, you must:

☑ **Enter Alpha or Theta.**
☑ **Engage the subconscious self with multi-sensory thought-forms.**
☑ **Use energy cultivation to amplify and transmit the request.**

This is the foundation of working **in harmony** with the subconscious self—**matching its frequency so it becomes a willing and active participant** in your manifestations.

In the next section, we will explore the **nature and characteristics of the subconscious self**—how it functions, how it processes emotions, and why building rapport with it is essential for success.

Section 3 – The Subconscious Self: Its Nature and Characteristics

By now, you understand that the subconscious self operates on a different **frequency** than the conscious self. But to truly work with it, you must also understand its **nature, characteristics, and motivations**.

Most people think of the subconscious as simply a **storage system** for memories, habits, and emotions. But in reality, it is a **living, intelligent part of you**—one that has its own way of thinking, reacting, and communicating.

The subconscious self is **not just a program running in the background**—it is a **conscious entity** with its own form of awareness. It is deeply loyal, highly impressionable, and incredibly powerful.

If the conscious self is like a **captain**, the subconscious self is the **crew**—it carries out instructions, but only if those instructions are **understood, accepted, and aligned** with its deeper programming.

Without training, the subconscious self **follows automatic patterns**, often shaped by **early childhood experiences, societal conditioning, and deep emotional imprints**.

The good news?
It can be re-trained.

And once you develop **rapport** with your subconscious self, it will **eagerly assist you** in achieving your goals—acting as a direct channel to the Transcendent Self.

The Subconscious Self's Primary Function: Serving the Other Selves
The subconscious self **exists to serve both the conscious self and the Transcendent Self**.

◈ It **listens to the conscious self** and follows its instructions—if those instructions are clear and emotionally charged.
◈ It **relays messages to the Transcendent Self**—but only if it is trained to do so.
◈ It **manages your body's energy, emotions, and involuntary functions**—acting as a bridge between the physical and non-physical.

In other words, the subconscious self is the **operator of the human system**.

But like any operator, it works best when it has:
✓ **Clear instructions** from the conscious self.

✓ **Trust in the captain (you).**
✓ **Enough energy to carry out its tasks.**

If the subconscious self is confused, depleted, or carrying unresolved trauma, it will **default to automatic survival patterns**, resisting change—even if that change is something the conscious self deeply desires.

The Role of the Subconscious Self in the Body

Unlike the conscious self, which is focused on **thoughts, decisions, and external actions**, the subconscious self is responsible for:

✓ **Regulating Involuntary Functions** – Heartbeat, digestion, immune response, and hormone balance.
✓ **Managing Energy Flow** – Distributing vital life force energy to different parts of the body.
✓ **Storing and Retrieving Memory** – Recording every sensory impression, thought, and experience.
✓ **Controlling Emotional Responses** – Determining how you react to situations based on past experiences.

This is why **manifestation is not just about thinking positively—** because **if the subconscious self is storing fear, doubt, or resistance**, those emotions will override your conscious desires.

The subconscious self does not think in **logic**—it operates through **associations, patterns, and emotions**.

For example:

- If you experienced **rejection as a child**, your subconscious self may form the belief: *"Success means being seen. Being seen means rejection. Rejection is painful. Therefore, success is dangerous."*

- Even if your conscious self desires success, your subconscious self will **resist it**—not out of malice, but out of **a deep-seated program designed to protect you from pain**.

This is why training the subconscious self is **critical**—because unless you **align it with your conscious desires**, it will unconsciously sabotage them.

The Subconscious Self and Its Unique Characteristics
◈ It Thinks in Symbols, Images, and Sensations

- The subconscious self does not use words—it communicates through **feelings, memories, and dreams**.

- This is why MSM uses **multi-sensory thought-forms**—because the subconscious responds to **vivid imagery and strong emotions**.

◈ It Takes Everything Literally

- The subconscious self does not understand sarcasm, jokes, or "empty" statements.

- If you say *"I'm terrible at this"* (even as a joke), your subconscious self **accepts it as a fact** and reinforces that belief.

- This is why using **deliberate, positive language** is essential when training the subconscious self.

◈ It Controls Emotional Reactions

- The subconscious self **stores emotional imprints** from past experiences, which trigger automatic responses in the present.

- This is why you may feel **anxiety, resistance, or fear** when trying something new—even if there is no logical reason for it.

- MSM helps **clear old emotional patterns** so the subconscious self stops running outdated programs.

◈ It Has No Concept of Time

- To the subconscious self, **past, present, and future all exist at once**.

- This is why old emotional wounds can still **affect you decades later**—because the subconscious is still holding onto them as if they are happening now.

- The good news? **This also means you can reprogram your past experiences and create a new future by shifting subconscious patterns.**

◈ **It Responds Best to Repetition**

- The subconscious self learns through **consistent reinforcement**.

- This is why **daily practices** like breathwork, visualization, and energy cultivation are key to manifestation—they create new patterns that the subconscious self can adopt.

Training the Subconscious Self to Work for You
Once you **understand how the subconscious self operates**, you can begin training it to **support** your conscious desires instead of resisting them.

In the next section, we will explore the **Aka Body**—the **energetic structure of the subconscious self**—and how **energetic cords connect us to people, places, and thought-forms**.

By working **with** these energetic structures, you will be able to:
✓ **Clear old energetic attachments that are influencing you.**
✓ **Strengthen your ability to send thought-forms to the Transcendent Self.**
✓ **Reprogram subconscious patterns at the deepest level.**

Because when you train the subconscious self to become **a willing and eager participant** in your manifestations, miracles stop feeling like chance events.

They become a **natural consequence of working with the true nature of reality.**

Section 4 – The Aka Body: The Energetic Structure of the Subconscious Self

The subconscious self is not just a collection of emotions, memories, and automatic processes—it also has a **distinct energetic structure** known as the **Aka Body**.

Understanding the Aka Body is critical in *Master the Science of Miracles*® because it explains **how energy moves, how thoughts are transmitted, and why past experiences continue to affect us energetically**.

By learning how to work with the Aka Body, you gain the ability to:
✓ **Strengthen your connection to the Transcendent Self.**
✓ **Clear negative energetic attachments that influence your subconscious programming.**
✓ **Increase the effectiveness of your multi-sensory thought-forms.**

The Aka Body: What Is It?

Ancient spiritual traditions, particularly in **Huna teachings**, describe the subconscious self as having a **shadowy, fluid-like body** that is separate from the physical form. This **Aka Body** (or "shadow body") is composed of **etheric substance**, a fine, invisible material that extends beyond the physical form.

Modern energy work aligns with this idea, recognizing the Aka Body as:

- **The energetic template of the subconscious self.**

- **The mechanism through which thought-forms and energy travel.**

- **The structure that connects us to people, places, memories, and events.**

Think of the Aka Body as **a web of invisible fibers** that extend from you and link you to everything you've ever interacted with.

Aka Cords: The Energetic Threads That Connect Us

Every time you interact with someone, think about a place, or even hold a strong emotional experience, you form an **Aka Cord**—an energetic thread that connects your Aka Body to that person, place, or thought.

These cords function as **highways for energy transmission**.

◈ **Strong emotional experiences create powerful Aka Cords.**

- If you have unresolved emotional ties to someone, the Aka Cord remains active, continuously influencing your subconscious self.

- This explains why some relationships feel "draining" even when the person is not physically present—your subconscious self is still **sending and receiving energy through the Aka Cord**.

◈ **Thought-forms and intentions travel along Aka Cords.**

- When you focus on a goal or visualize an outcome, your thought-form is **delivered to the Transcendent Self along an Aka Cord**.

- This is why MSM emphasizes **clear, structured, high-energy thought-forms**—because the more refined and powerful the thought, the more effective the transmission.

◈ **Aka Cords are non-local—they operate beyond space and time.**

- Once a connection is formed, it remains intact unless consciously cleared.

- This is why someone you haven't spoken to in years can suddenly **come to mind, call you, or appear in your dreams**—because the Aka Cord is still active.

The Aka Body and its Aka Cords explain many **unexplainable phenomena**—such as telepathy, sudden intuitive insights, and why unresolved emotional wounds continue to affect us long after an event has passed.

Quantum Science and Aka Cords

Modern physics offers an intriguing parallel to the Aka Cord concept—**Quantum Entanglement**.

In simple terms, quantum entanglement shows that when two particles become linked, a change in one instantly affects the other **no matter how far apart they are**.

This mirrors the idea that Aka Cords allow **instantaneous energy transmission**—whether it's between people, thought-forms, or even past and future events.

✓ Energy is not bound by time or space.
✓ Once a connection is formed, energy flows instantly between two points.
✓ Your subconscious self uses this system to transmit desires, emotions, and thought-forms to the Transcendent Self.

By working **consciously** with Aka Cords, you can **refine your energy connections**, clear outdated attachments, and **enhance the precision of your manifestations**.

Clearing and Strengthening Aka Cords

Most people go through life **unaware of the energetic cords they carry,** allowing old emotional wounds, past relationships, and stagnant beliefs to **drain their energy and distort their manifestations**.

To ensure your subconscious self is **operating at peak efficiency**, it's essential to:

1 **Clear Aka Cords that are no longer serving you.**

- Cut or dissolve cords connected to **past trauma, negative relationships, or limiting beliefs.**

2 **Strengthen the Aka Cords that empower you.**

- Reinforce your connection to the **Transcendent Self**, goals, and high-vibration thought-forms.

3 **Keep your energy field clear.**

- Regular breathwork, meditation, and visualization practices help **remove stagnant Aka residue** and keep energy flowing freely.

This is why MSM incorporates **energy-clearing techniques**—to ensure your Aka Body is **functioning as a precise, effective transmission system** rather than an **unconscious energy drain**.

Applying This Knowledge in MSM

Understanding the Aka Body is essential for:

✓ **Training the subconscious self to send clear thought-forms to the Transcendent Self.**

✓ **Releasing subconscious blocks tied to outdated Aka Cords.**

✓ **Increasing the speed and accuracy of manifestation.**

In the next section, we will explore **the role of emotions in subconscious programming**—how **emotions shape your Aka Cords**, and why working with emotions is the fastest way to reprogram the subconscious self for success.

Because **if energy is the fuel, emotions are the ignition**—and mastering this relationship is key to becoming a deliberate creator of miracles.

Section 5 – Emotions: The Language of the Subconscious Self

If **energy is the fuel** of the subconscious self, then **emotions are the ignition switch**.

Most people believe they control their emotions, but in reality, the subconscious self **controls and administers all emotional responses**. Every feeling—love, joy, fear, grief, excitement—is regulated by the subconscious self based on **past experiences and ingrained patterns**.

This is why people often find themselves **reacting emotionally** in ways they don't understand. Their conscious self might want to remain calm, but their subconscious self is operating on **a deeply ingrained emotional program**.

To master *Master the Science of Miracles®*, you must learn how to **work with emotions rather than be controlled by them**.

Because **it is emotions—not logic—that drive the subconscious self.**

The Subconscious Self as the Source of Emotions

The subconscious self is constantly processing experiences and translating them into **emotional signals**.

These signals serve two main purposes:

1 **To protect you from perceived danger**

- The subconscious self will trigger **fear, anxiety, or resistance** if it perceives something as a **threat based on past experiences**.

- This explains why someone might feel **afraid of success** or **resistant to change**, even when their conscious self logically knows the change is positive.

72

2 **To reinforce what it believes is beneficial**

- If an experience **aligns with a positive emotional memory**, the subconscious self will **generate joy, excitement, or attraction** to encourage repetition.

- This is why certain environments, smells, or songs can **evoke deep feelings of comfort or happiness**—the subconscious self has linked them to past positive experiences.

The key takeaway?
✓ **Emotions are the subconscious self's primary way of communicating.**

If you want to train the subconscious self, you must **speak its language**—and that language is **emotionally charged experiences**.

How Thought and Emotion Work Together
Most people assume **thought comes first**, followed by emotion.

In reality, the **subconscious self generates emotions first**, and those emotions **influence the conscious thoughts that follow**.

For example:

- If the subconscious self **associates money with security**, the idea of wealth will trigger **relaxation, confidence, and optimism**.

- If the subconscious self **associates money with stress**, the idea of wealth will trigger **fear, worry, or avoidance**—even if the conscious self desires financial success.

This is why many people experience **conflict between their conscious desires and their emotional responses**—because their subconscious self is running an **outdated emotional program** that contradicts their goals.

To **align the subconscious self with your desired reality**, you must **reprogram the emotional responses connected to it**.

The Emotional Blueprint of the Subconscious Self
Every major experience in your life has been stored in your subconscious self **alongside an emotional charge**.

◈ **Positive experiences = Energetic Reinforcement**

- If a childhood experience reinforced **love, confidence, or empowerment**, the subconscious self **seeks to repeat** those experiences.

◈ **Negative experiences = Emotional Barriers**

- If a painful experience reinforced **fear, rejection, or unworthiness**, the subconscious self will **actively avoid** situations that might repeat that pain—even if avoiding them prevents growth.

The subconscious self is **not trying to sabotage you**—it is simply **following its programming**.

The good news?
That programming can be rewritten.

Reprogramming Emotional Responses for Manifestation
Since the subconscious self **responds to emotions more than logic**, the fastest way to influence it is through **emotionally charged multi-sensory thought-forms**.

This means that when sending thought-forms to the Transcendent Self, you must:

✓ **Feel as if the outcome is already real.**
✓ **Generate the emotions you would have if it had already**

happened.
✓ **Flood the subconscious self with emotional certainty.**

This **bypasses doubt and resistance** because the subconscious self **accepts emotionally charged experiences as reality**.

Why MSM Uses Emotional Charging
In MSM, a thought-form without emotional charge is weak.

The subconscious self must be fully **engaged and emotionally invested** for a thought-form to be successfully transmitted to the Transcendent Self.

This is why MSM includes:

✅ **Peak State Exercises** – Activating powerful emotional memories to **raise your vibration before manifestation work**.
✅ **Anchoring Techniques** – Associating a physical trigger (like a hand gesture or deep breath) with positive emotions to **instantly shift your state**.
✅ **Multi-Sensory Thought-Form Creation** – Ensuring **sight, sound, feeling, and energy** are embedded into every manifestation practice.

By working with the **subconscious self's natural language of emotions**, MSM ensures that **manifestation is not just an intellectual exercise—but an immersive, emotionally charged experience.**

Shifting the Emotional Blueprint of the Subconscious Self
To truly align the subconscious self with **effortless manifestation**, you must:

1 Clear Negative Emotional Associations

- Identify and release emotional barriers **linked to your desires**.

- Example: If money triggers anxiety, work on **releasing old financial trauma**.

2 **Anchor High-Vibration Emotional States**

- Train the subconscious self to associate your goals with **joy, excitement, and ease**.

- Example: If love has been painful in the past, anchor **feelings of safety, love, and connection** to future relationships.

3 **Reinforce New Emotional Patterns Through Repetition**

- The subconscious self **learns through consistent reinforcement**—daily MSM practices are essential.

- Example: Practicing **emotional rehearsal** by feeling gratitude, success, and joy every day trains the subconscious to **accept those emotions as default states**.

When you train the subconscious self to associate **your desires with positive emotional states**, manifestation becomes **effortless, natural, and automatic**.

Applying This Knowledge in MSM
Emotions are the **fastest way to access and reprogram the subconscious self**.

In the next section, we will explore **how the subconscious self manages vital life force energy**—and why **energy and emotion must work together** for manifestation to succeed.

Because **emotion directs energy, and energy fuels manifestation**—and when these forces are aligned, miracles happen.

Section 6 – The Subconscious Self and Vital Life Force Energy

At this point, you understand that the subconscious self operates through **emotion**—but there is another equally important factor: **energy**.

If **emotion is the ignition switch** of the subconscious self, then **vital life force energy is the fuel that makes manifestation possible**.

The subconscious self is the **administrator and regulator of energy flow** throughout your system. It **gathers, stores, and directs** energy where it is needed most. This means that the amount of energy you have available directly affects:

✓ **Your physical health and vitality**
✓ **Your emotional stability and mental clarity**
✓ **Your ability to manifest thought-forms into reality**

Without an **excess charge of vital life force energy**, even the most vividly imagined multi-sensory thought-forms will lack the power to reach the Transcendent Self. This is why **energy cultivation is a core component of MSM**—because without energy, there is no transformation.

The Subconscious Self as the Energy Manager

The subconscious self is responsible for **four key energy functions**:

1 **Absorbing Energy** – Collecting life force energy from breath, food, sunlight, and the environment.
2 **Storing Energy** – Holding excess energy in the **Lower Dan Tian**, the body's primary energy reservoir.
3 **Distributing Energy** – Sending energy to the body's organs, emotions, and thought-forms.
4 **Projecting Energy** – Transmitting energy outward, either consciously (as in MSM techniques) or unconsciously.

Most people are **unaware of their subconscious self's role** in managing energy, which means they **leak energy constantly**—leaving them feeling drained, unfocused, and unable to manifest effectively.

By training the subconscious self to **hold and direct energy deliberately**, you create a **high-powered manifestation system** capable of turning thought into reality with precision.

Why Most People Operate with Low Energy

The subconscious self does not naturally prioritize manifestation—it prioritizes **survival**.

If energy levels are low, the subconscious self will **redirect energy toward bodily functions and emotional regulation** rather than manifestation.

Common **energy drains** include:
✘ **Negative emotions** – Fear, anger, stress, and anxiety consume massive amounts of energy.
✘ **Overthinking** – Excessive mental chatter burns energy without producing results.
✘ **Environmental toxins and poor diet** – The subconscious self must use energy to detoxify the body.
✘ **Lack of breath awareness** – Shallow breathing limits oxygen intake and energy absorption.

When the subconscious self is **constantly using energy just to maintain basic functions**, it has little left to **fuel thought-forms and send them to the Transcendent Self.**

This is why energy cultivation is not **optional** in MSM—it is a **fundamental requirement**.

Breathwork: The Fastest Way to Recharge the Subconscious Self

The easiest and most effective way to train the subconscious self to

store an excess charge of energy is through **conscious breathing techniques**.

Breathwork allows you to:
✓ **Absorb more life force energy.**
✓ **Train the subconscious self to store energy in the Lower Dan Tian.**
✓ **Increase the amount of energy available for thought-form transmission.**

Each time you **breathe consciously and deeply**, the subconscious self **registers that it is safe to hold an excess charge of energy** rather than depleting it for survival functions.

This is why MSM includes:
☑ **Lower Dan Tian Breathing** – Strengthening the body's energy reservoir.
☑ **Standing Energy Cultivation** – Activating and circulating energy through movement.
☑ **Energy Projection Exercises** – Training the subconscious self to direct energy outward with precision.

When the subconscious self consistently **holds an excess charge of energy**, manifestation becomes **exponentially more effective—** because now, the **thought-form has the power it needs to reach the Transcendent Self.**

The Relationship Between Energy and Emotion
Energy and emotion **are not separate forces**—they are deeply intertwined.

◈ **High-vibration emotions like joy, love, and gratitude increase energy flow.**
◈ **Low-vibration emotions like fear, worry, and shame drain energy rapidly.**

This is why MSM teaches students to:
✓ **Consciously generate high-energy emotions when creating**

thought-forms.

✓ Use breathwork to prevent emotional energy from depleting the system.

✓ Clear subconscious blocks that siphon energy unconsciously.

If the subconscious self is **fully charged with energy AND emotionally aligned with a desire**, the thought-form becomes **unstoppable**.

The Final Step: Directing Energy for Manifestation

Once the subconscious self:

☑ **Holds an excess charge of energy**

☑ **Is emotionally aligned with a desired outcome**

☑ **Is trained to send energy outward**

...then the final step is **deliberately directing that energy into a multi-sensory thought-form and transmitting it to the Transcendent Self**.

In the next section, we will explore **the subconscious self as the gateway to memory**—and why reprogramming stored memories is one of the most effective ways to accelerate transformation.

Because **memory shapes identity, and identity determines what you allow yourself to manifest**.

Key Takeaways from This Section

💡 The **subconscious self manages vital life force energy**—absorbing, storing, distributing, and projecting it.

💡 **Low energy levels make manifestation difficult** because the subconscious self prioritizes survival over transformation.

💡 **Breathwork is the fastest way to train the subconscious self to hold an excess charge of energy.**

💡 **Emotion and energy must work together**—emotion directs energy, and energy fuels manifestation.

When you master these principles, **you stop struggling with manifestation**—because your subconscious self is now **a fully charged, trained energy system capable of turning thought into reality.**

Section 7 – The Subconscious Self as the Gateway to Memory

Memory is the **foundation of identity**.

Everything you believe about yourself, your abilities, and your reality is shaped by **the memories stored in your subconscious self**. These memories don't just sit passively in your mind—they **actively shape your perception, emotional responses, and ability to manifest.**

If your subconscious self **associates success with struggle**, it will resist effortless achievement.
If it **associates money with conflict**, it will create financial obstacles.
If it **associates love with pain**, it will push away fulfilling relationships.

Most people **don't realize that their memories are affecting their manifestations**—because they assume that memories are static, unchangeable records of the past.

But here's the truth:
Memories are fluid, living imprints within the subconscious self, and they can be reprogrammed.

By learning how to **consciously interact with and reshape memories**, you can train your subconscious self to **align with your highest desires rather than work against them.**

How the Subconscious Self Stores and Retrieves Memory

The subconscious self is **the ultimate record keeper**—it **remembers everything** you've ever experienced, from birth to the present moment.

Unlike the conscious self, which can only focus on **one thought at a time**, the subconscious self processes **billions of sensory impressions simultaneously** and organizes them into **clusters of related memories**.

◈ Memories Are Stored in Associative Clusters

- Think of memory as a **grapevine**—one thought triggers a **chain reaction**, leading to a network of associated emotions, past experiences, and beliefs.

- This is why a single smell, sound, or phrase can **suddenly bring back a flood of emotions** from the past.

◈ Emotional Intensity Determines How Deeply a Memory is Imprinted

- Memories that carry **strong emotional energy** (whether positive or negative) are **more deeply embedded** in the subconscious self.

- This is why traumatic events **can feel more real than everyday experiences**, even decades later.

◈ The Subconscious Self Does Not Recognize Time

- To the subconscious self, **all memories exist in the present moment**.

- This is why **past emotional wounds can still trigger present-day reactions**—because the subconscious self does not distinguish between *then* and *now*.

If a memory **carries an emotional charge**, the subconscious self **acts as if it is still happening**, influencing your thoughts, emotions, and behaviors **in the present**.

How Memory Blocks Manifestation

If your subconscious self is **storing unprocessed emotions** from past experiences, those emotions **can override your conscious intentions**, preventing successful manifestation.

For example:

✗ **Financial Manifestation Block** – If your subconscious self **remembers** moments of financial struggle from childhood, it may associate money with **fear, lack, or family conflict**, making financial success feel "unsafe."

✗ **Love & Relationships Block** – If your subconscious self **remembers** a painful heartbreak, it may associate love with **rejection, betrayal, or loss**, leading to unconscious self-sabotage in new relationships.

✗ **Success & Visibility Block** – If your subconscious self **remembers** being ridiculed or judged for standing out, it may associate success with **shame, embarrassment, or rejection**, causing procrastination or fear of being seen.

In each case, the subconscious self is not **trying to block you**—it is simply **protecting you from repeating a perceived danger.**

This is why manifestation doesn't always work the way people expect. If your subconscious self **associates your desire with pain, fear, or loss**, it will prevent that desire from becoming reality.

Reprogramming Memory for Manifestation

The good news?

Because memories are **not static**, they can be **re-coded and reinterpreted**—allowing you to **change the emotional charge associated with them.**

By consciously working with memory, you can:
✓ **Transform past trauma into empowerment.**
✓ **Dissolve emotional blocks that prevent manifestation.**
✓ **Train your subconscious self to view success, love, and abundance as safe and natural.**

The subconscious self does not respond to **logic**—it responds to **emotion and sensory experience**. This means that to reprogram a memory, you must **emotionally engage with it in a new way**.

The MSM Memory Reprogramming Process

To train the subconscious self to **release old limitations and align with new realities**, MSM uses a structured **memory reprogramming process**:

1 Recall the Memory

- Close your eyes and bring up the **earliest memory** associated with a limiting belief.

- Let the scene **come into focus**, allowing yourself to feel its emotional charge.

2 Step Outside the Experience

- Imagine watching the memory as if it were a **scene in a movie.**

- Instead of **reliving the emotion**, observe it **from a detached perspective**.

3 Introduce a New Interpretation

- Ask yourself: *What was the lesson hidden in this experience?*

- Shift your perspective to see how this event actually **prepared you for something greater**.

4 Alter the Sensory Imprint

- Change the memory's **color, brightness, or intensity—** softening harsh details.

- Add **supportive figures** (a mentor, a higher self, or an angelic presence) into the scene.

- Imagine the past version of yourself **receiving comfort, wisdom, or strength** from this presence.

5 Reimprint the Emotion

- Take a deep breath and **bring in a new emotion**—peace, empowerment, gratitude.

- Imagine this **new emotion flooding the memory**, rewriting its meaning in your subconscious self.

6 Anchor the New Pattern

- Open your eyes and **physically reinforce the new belief** (through a deep breath, a smile, or a verbal affirmation).

- Repeat the process until the **emotional charge of the old memory is fully neutralized**.

This process **trains the subconscious self to release outdated patterns**, replacing them with **high-vibration emotional states that align with manifestation success**.

The Power of Memory in Shaping Reality
Memory is not just a record of the past—it is an **active force shaping your future**.

When you **clear and reprogram memory**, you unlock the ability to:
✓ **Manifest without resistance** because the subconscious self is no longer blocking your desires.
✓ **Stay emotionally aligned with your goals** rather than being unconsciously pulled into old patterns.
✓ **Strengthen your connection to the Transcendent Self**, allowing manifestations to flow effortlessly.

In the next section, we will explore **how the subconscious self evolves over time**—and why training it to move beyond survival instincts is key to unlocking your highest potential.

Because **you are not limited by your past—unless you allow yourself to be.**

When you rewrite your memories, **you rewrite your reality.**

Key Takeaways from This Section

💡 The subconscious self stores all memories, organizing them into emotional clusters.

💡 Memories are fluid and can be reprogrammed to dissolve limiting beliefs.

💡 Emotional imprints from past experiences shape your present manifestations.

💡 The subconscious self does not recognize time—old memories still affect you unless consciously reprocessed.

💡 MSM uses structured memory reprogramming to clear subconscious blocks and create alignment.

When you take control of **how your subconscious self interprets past experiences**, you step into **a new level of manifestation mastery**—where past wounds no longer dictate your future.

Section 8 – The Evolution of the Subconscious Self

The subconscious self is not static.

It is not a fixed set of programs, running the same patterns for life. Instead, it is **fluid, adaptable, and capable of evolving**—if given the right training.

Most people assume that their subconscious self is permanently shaped by childhood experiences, cultural conditioning, or past trauma. But the truth is, the subconscious self **can be refined, upgraded, and evolved into a more advanced state**—one that fully supports manifestation, spiritual growth, and higher consciousness.

The evolution of the subconscious self is the missing piece in many manifestation systems.

✓ If the subconscious self remains **stuck in survival mode**, it will continue operating from fear, limitation, and past conditioning.
✓ If the subconscious self is **trained to evolve**, it begins aligning with **higher states of consciousness, effortless manifestation, and deep intuition**.

The key to achieving this evolution lies in **recognizing where your subconscious self is operating from—and shifting it into a higher mode of functioning.**

How the Subconscious Self Evolves Over Time
In psychology, the evolution of human consciousness has been mapped in many ways—from Freud's model of the psyche to Jung's individuation process to Maslow's Hierarchy of Needs.

Each of these models recognizes one thing:
Humans grow in stages, and their subconscious programming must evolve along with them.

Maslow's **Hierarchy of Needs** provides a useful framework for understanding how the subconscious self matures:

1 **Survival Stage (Base Level)**

- The subconscious self is focused on **physical safety, food, shelter, and survival**.

- Energy is used for **self-preservation**, not manifestation.

- At this stage, manifestation seems **impossible** because the subconscious self is operating in **constant stress mode**.

2 Emotional Security & Belonging Stage

- The subconscious self prioritizes **emotional connection, relationships, and social acceptance**.

- Manifestation is possible, but only within the framework of **what feels emotionally safe**.

- Limiting beliefs often stem from this stage (e.g., fear of rejection, need for validation).

3 Self-Actualization Stage

- The subconscious self begins supporting **personal growth, confidence, and high-level goals**.

- Manifestation accelerates because the subconscious self is no longer **fighting against change**.

- Thought-forms become clearer, more potent, and more aligned with the Transcendent Self.

4 Self-Transcendence Stage (Highest Evolution)

- The subconscious self becomes an **open channel for divine intelligence**.

- Manifestation moves beyond personal desires into **service, purpose, and alignment with higher consciousness**.

- At this level, the subconscious self fully **harmonizes with the Transcendent Self**, allowing miracles to flow effortlessly.

The subconscious self's **evolution is not automatic**—it must be **deliberately guided and trained**.

Most people are stuck **operating at the lower two stages**, unable to manifest because their subconscious self is still programmed for **survival and emotional security**.

To evolve into the **higher stages**, you must train the subconscious self to:
✓ **Move beyond survival-based fears.**

✓ Let go of outdated emotional patterns.
✓ Develop a direct relationship with the Transcendent Self.

This process requires **deliberate reprogramming**, which MSM provides through specific techniques designed to **shift the subconscious self into higher-functioning states**.

Training the Subconscious Self to Evolve
The subconscious self is **always learning**—but it learns through **experience, repetition, and reinforcement**.

To shift into a **higher state of operation**, it must be trained through:

✓ **Daily Energy Cultivation** – Increasing the subconscious self's ability to **hold and direct energy** beyond survival needs.
✓ **Emotional Reprogramming** – Releasing fear-based emotional patterns that keep it locked in past conditioning.
✓ **Multi-Sensory Thought-Form Creation** – Training the subconscious self to expect **miracles as the new normal**.
✓ **Higher-Level Identity Shifting** – Teaching the subconscious self to embody **a new identity aligned with its highest evolution**.

When the subconscious self evolves, **everything in life becomes easier**—manifestation, relationships, intuition, even physical health.

Instead of **resisting transformation**, the subconscious self **actively supports and amplifies it**.

Why This Evolution is Essential for MSM Success
If you've ever felt like **manifestation works sometimes, but not consistently**, it is because your subconscious self is **still transitioning between evolutionary stages**.

At lower levels, the subconscious self **fears change and clings to past limitations**.

At higher levels, the subconscious self **embraces change and seeks growth as its natural state**.

The subconscious self **must be trained to reach and stay in the higher stages**—otherwise, it will revert back to **old, survival-based patterns** the moment a challenge arises.

This is why MSM provides a **step-by-step process for reprogramming the subconscious self**.

The Subconscious Self and Its Role in Spiritual Awakening

When fully trained and evolved, the subconscious self becomes **a bridge to higher consciousness**.

It no longer operates as **a reactive, fear-based entity**—instead, it becomes a **cooperative partner in spiritual awakening**.

At this level, the subconscious self begins to:

✓ **Enhance intuitive perception.**
✓ **Generate excess energy to fuel multi-sensory thought-forms.**
✓ **Transmute fear-based emotions into higher states of awareness.**
✓ **Effortlessly transmit requests to the Transcendent Self.**

This is when miracles stop being **occasional events** and start being **a daily experience**.

When your subconscious self evolves to its **highest state**, manifestation becomes **second nature**, and you begin operating in **harmony with universal intelligence**.

Preparing for the Final Phases of Subconscious Training

By now, you understand that the subconscious self is not an **obstacle**—it is a **partner in creation**.

In the next section, we will explore **how to develop a direct relationship with the subconscious self**—learning to **communicate with it, listen to its guidance, and refine its abilities for manifestation.**

Because when you **train your subconscious self to be your greatest ally,** you step into a **completely new reality—one where the energy of miracles flows effortlessly through you.**

Key Takeaways from This Section

💡 The subconscious self **evolves in stages**, moving from survival-based fears to higher consciousness.

💡 Most people's subconscious selves are **stuck in outdated survival patterns**, limiting their ability to manifest.

💡 Training the subconscious self allows it to **support rather than resist manifestation**.

💡 A fully evolved subconscious self **operates as a bridge to the Transcendent Self**, allowing for effortless miracles.

When you master the evolution of your subconscious self, **you unlock the highest level of manifestation and spiritual awareness possible.**

Section 9 – The Art of Getting Acquainted with Your Subconscious Self

By now, you understand that the subconscious self is not just an automatic program running in the background of your mind—it is a **living, intelligent part of you** that plays a **crucial role in manifestation, energy management, and emotional regulation**.

But for most people, the subconscious self remains a **mystery**—an unseen force that influences their lives without their conscious awareness.

To fully integrate *Master the Science of Miracles®*, you must go beyond merely **understanding** the subconscious self—you must develop a **direct relationship** with it.

When you establish **rapport** with your subconscious self, everything changes:
✓ Your manifestations become more precise and effective.
✓ Emotional and energetic resistance decreases.
✓ You gain **access to deep intuition, hidden memories, and powerful insights.**

Most importantly, the subconscious self stops being an **unconscious obstacle** and becomes **a fully cooperative partner in creation**.

The first step? **Introducing yourself to your subconscious self—formally, directly, and with intention.**

Why Some People Struggle to Connect with Their Subconscious Self

The subconscious self is always listening and always responding—but most people have spent years ignoring or misunderstanding its messages.

◈ **They were never taught that it exists as a separate intelligence.**
◈ **They have spent years suppressing emotions, disconnecting from their inner world.**
◈ **They unknowingly created subconscious resistance through negative self-talk or doubt.**

If the subconscious self has been ignored, scolded, or neglected for years, it may not immediately respond to attempts at communication.

Just like a person who has been shut out of a conversation for years, it may initially remain **silent, hesitant, or resistant.**

But with **gentleness, patience, and consistent practice**, the subconscious self can become **highly responsive**—eager to communicate and assist you in your manifestations.

The key is to **start the relationship on the right foot**—with **respect, openness, and clear intention.**

How to Initiate Contact with Your Subconscious Self
To build a strong connection, you must **speak the language of the subconscious self**—which is **emotion, imagery, and energy** rather than logic or force.

Try this **simple exercise** to begin developing rapport:

1 **Find a Quiet Space**

- Sit comfortably in a place where you won't be disturbed.

- Take a few deep breaths, allowing your body to relax.

2 **Acknowledge the Presence of Your Subconscious Self**

- Close your eyes and **bring awareness to your inner world**.

- Silently or aloud, say:
  "I know you are here, and I want to connect with you."

- Don't force a response—simply acknowledge its existence.

3 **Listen for a Response**

- Pay attention to any **subtle sensations, emotions, or images** that arise.

- The subconscious self does not communicate in words—it responds with **feelings, memories, or dream-like impressions.**

- Be patient—if nothing happens immediately, that's okay. The act of reaching out **initiates the process of opening the connection.**

4 **Ask a Simple Question**

- You can ask something like:
  "What do you need me to know right now?" or *"How can I strengthen our connection?"*

- Allow your subconscious self to **respond in its own way— through emotions, visual impressions, or physical sensations.**

5 **Thank Your Subconscious Self**

- Whether you receive a response or not, **express gratitude** for its presence.

- The subconscious self, like any intelligent being, responds positively to appreciation.

Practicing this exercise **daily** signals to the subconscious self that you are serious about developing communication. Over time, the responses will become **clearer, stronger, and more intuitive.**

Recognizing Subconscious Communication

Once you initiate this connection, your subconscious self will begin **sending signals** in various ways.

✓ **Through Dreams** – The subconscious self often communicates through symbolic dream imagery.
✓ **Through Sudden Intuition** – A gut feeling or instant knowing is often a **direct response** from the subconscious self.
✓ **Through Emotions** – Sudden shifts in mood or energy can indicate **subconscious guidance or resistance**.
✓ **Through Body Sensations** – Tension, relaxation, or warmth in specific areas of the body may be **physical responses from the subconscious self.**

Becoming aware of these **signals** strengthens your ability to recognize when your subconscious self is trying to communicate with you.

Deepening the Connection Through Writing

Another powerful way to build rapport is through **automatic writing**.

This involves setting aside **five minutes a day** to write whatever comes to mind without judgment.

Try this process:

1 **Begin with a Simple Prompt**

- Write: *"Subconscious self, what do you want to tell me today?"*
  2 Write Freely Without Editing

- Let the words flow without overthinking.
  3 Look for Patterns Over Time

- The more you practice, the clearer the subconscious responses will become.

This practice **bypasses the critical mind** and allows the subconscious self to communicate in a **fluid, direct way.**

The Importance of Respecting the Subconscious Self

The subconscious self is not a machine—it is an **intelligent, emotional, and deeply loyal part of you.**

✓ **It does not respond to force—it responds to trust.**
✓ **It does not function well under pressure—it thrives on patience.**
✓ **It will not work against you if treated with respect—it will become your greatest ally.**

Building a strong relationship with your subconscious self is **not a one-time event—it is an ongoing practice.**

The more you listen, acknowledge, and honor it, the more **it will work with you instead of against you.**

Preparing for Advanced Subconscious Training

Now that you've begun **establishing communication**, the next step is to **train the subconscious self to actively participate in manifestation.**

In the next section, we will explore **the first structured exercise for subconscious training—the Pendulum Exercise**—which will teach you how to receive clear, verifiable responses from your subconscious self in real-time.

Because when your subconscious self is no longer just a hidden force but **an active participant in your manifestations**, miracles become a **reliable and repeatable process.**

Key Takeaways from This Section

💡 **The subconscious self is an intelligent being that can be engaged as a partner.**

💡 **Most people struggle to connect because they have ignored or misunderstood their subconscious self.**

💡 **Simple exercises—like acknowledging its presence, listening for signals, and practicing automatic writing—help build rapport.**

💡 **Developing trust and communication makes manifestation easier, faster, and more precise.**

When you train your subconscious self to be **a conscious co-creator**, you no longer need to **fight for your manifestations**—you simply **align with them, and they unfold naturally.**

Section 10 – Phase 2: Training the Subconscious Self

Now that you have begun developing **rapport with your subconscious self**, the next step is to **train it to become a reliable and active participant in manifestation.**

This phase moves beyond simply **recognizing the subconscious self's influence**—you are now teaching it to:
✔ **Respond to direct communication.**
✔ **Assist in decision-making with clarity and precision.**
✔ **Strengthen its ability to send thought-forms to the Transcendent Self.**

The subconscious self is highly **trainable**, but it must be **taught through experience**—not just concepts.

This is where **structured exercises** come into play.

The first training tool? **The Pendulum Exercise.**

Introducing the Pendulum Exercise
The **Pendulum Exercise** is one of the simplest and most effective ways to begin training the subconscious self to:
✔ **Provide direct responses to questions.**
✔ **Increase its ability to follow commands.**
✔ **Strengthen its influence over physical energy flow.**

This exercise is **not about external forces or mystical guidance**—it is a method of communicating with **your own subconscious self** using micro-muscular responses.

When the subconscious self **accepts a question and decides on an answer**, it subtly influences the **involuntary muscles in your hand**, causing the pendulum to move.

This allows you to receive **clear, verifiable yes/no responses from your subconscious self in real time.**

Over time, this practice trains the subconscious self to:
✔ **Become more precise in its responses.**
✔ **Strengthen its ability to direct physical energy.**
✔ **Increase cooperation with the conscious and Transcendent Self.**

Setting Up the Pendulum Exercise
Step 1: Choose Your Pendulum

You don't need a store-bought pendulum—any small weighted object on a string will work.

✓ A ring, button, or small crystal tied to a piece of string.
✓ A lightweight pendant or chain.

The **subconscious self does not care about the object**—it only needs a way to express movement.

Step 2: Find a Quiet Space

- Sit comfortably at a table or desk.

- Rest your elbow on the surface so that your hand can dangle freely.

- Hold the pendulum between your thumb and forefinger, allowing it to hang still.

Step 3: Establish a Communication System

The subconscious self needs to **learn how to move the pendulum in a predictable way**.

1 Ask for a YES Response

- Say aloud: *"Subconscious self, please show me YES."*

- Wait patiently—after a few moments, the pendulum will **begin moving in a specific direction** (back and forth, side to side, or in a circle).

- Once it stabilizes, **note the movement**—this is now your YES response.

2 Ask for a NO Response

- Say aloud: *"Subconscious self, please show me NO."*

- The pendulum will move **differently than before**—this is your NO response.

3 Ask for a NEUTRAL Response

- Say aloud: *"Subconscious self, please show me a NEUTRAL response."*

- The pendulum will either remain still or show a slight, undefined movement.

Step 4: Practice Asking Simple Questions

Now that the subconscious self has established YES and NO movements, you can begin training with easy, verifiable questions:

☑ *"Is my name [your name]?"* → (Pendulum should move to YES.)
☑ *"Is today [wrong day of the week]?"* → (Pendulum should move to NO.)

By starting with **clear, factual questions**, you train the subconscious self to provide **accurate and consistent responses**.

Using the Pendulum for Subconscious Training

Once the subconscious self **understands the exercise**, you can begin using the pendulum to:

✓ **Strengthen trust and cooperation with the subconscious self.**
✓ **Test for subconscious resistance to goals.**
✓ **Verify whether the subconscious self is aligned with a specific manifestation.**

Try these training exercises:

◈ Reinforcing Positive Alignment

- Ask: *"Do you support my goal of financial abundance?"*

- If the response is YES, your subconscious self is aligned.

- If the response is NO, it indicates **hidden resistance** that needs to be addressed.

◈ Clearing Emotional Blocks

- Ask: *"Do I have unresolved fear around success?"*

- If the response is YES, it signals a subconscious block that can be cleared through MSM techniques.

◈ Energy Sensitivity Training

- Hold the pendulum over different areas of the body and ask: *"Is my Lower Dan Tian energy strong?"*

- The pendulum's response will indicate **where energy is flowing freely and where blockages may exist**.

This exercise **strengthens the subconscious self's ability to communicate directly**, increasing its responsiveness and cooperation.

Strengthening the Subconscious Self's Influence Over Reality
The **Pendulum Exercise** is only the beginning.

As the subconscious self becomes **more trained and responsive**, its ability to:
✔ **Direct vital life force energy** increases.
✔ **Transmute emotions into power** improves.
✔ **Effortlessly send multi-sensory thought-forms to the Transcendent Self** becomes second nature.

Training the subconscious self through **structured exercises like this** is what separates random success from **deliberate, reliable manifestation**.

Preparing for Advanced Subconscious Training
Now that you have learned to **engage the subconscious self directly**, the next phase of training will involve:
✔ **Strengthening subconscious energy control.**

✓ Reinforcing the ability to hold an excess charge of energy.
✓ Refining communication for deeper insights and accuracy.

In the next section, we will explore how to **expand beyond basic pendulum training** and strengthen the subconscious self's **ability to respond to commands, refine thought-forms, and accelerate manifestation.**

Because once your subconscious self is **fully trained**, manifestation stops being a struggle—it becomes a **precision process powered by an intelligent subconscious system.**

Key Takeaways from This Section
💡 The subconscious self can be trained to give direct, verifiable responses.
💡 The Pendulum Exercise teaches the subconscious self to communicate clearly and reliably.
💡 Once trained, the subconscious self can verify alignment, identify resistance, and strengthen energy flow.
💡 This exercise is the foundation for advanced subconscious training, allowing for greater precision in manifestation.

When your subconscious self becomes **a disciplined, responsive partner**, you no longer **hope for results—you create them with certainty.**

Section 11 – Strengthening Communication with the Subconscious Self

Now that you have established **direct contact with your subconscious self** through the **Pendulum Exercise**, the next step is to **refine and strengthen** this communication.

The subconscious self is like a **loyal but underutilized assistant**—it has always been working behind the scenes, but now that it has been given direct instructions, it must be **trained for precision, reliability, and expanded functionality**.

To deepen your ability to work with the subconscious self, you must:
✓ **Expand beyond simple yes/no responses.**
✓ **Develop a feedback system that allows for more detailed insights.**
✓ **Reinforce the subconscious self's role as an active partner in manifestation.**

This phase of training moves beyond **basic communication** and into **subconscious mastery**, ensuring that your subconscious self not only responds but **actively supports and enhances** your manifestations.

Beyond Yes/No: Expanding the Subconscious Feedback System
While the **Pendulum Exercise** is an excellent starting point, its limitation is that it only provides **binary (yes/no) answers**.

To deepen communication, you must **train the subconscious self to provide more nuanced feedback**.

Here are three effective ways to **expand subconscious communication**:

1. Using Percentage Scales for Precision

Instead of simply asking **"Yes" or "No,"** you can refine the subconscious response by introducing **percentage-based answers**:

✅ **Example:** *"To what degree is my subconscious self aligned with my goal of financial freedom?"*

- Instead of a **yes/no answer**, establish **10% increments** on the pendulum's movement.

- The subconscious self can then **indicate 30%, 50%, 80%, or 100% alignment**.

- This method allows you to see **where subconscious resistance exists** and how much more alignment is needed.

2. Testing Different Scenarios

You can use the pendulum to evaluate different choices by testing **multiple options** rather than just "Yes" or "No."

✅ **Example:** *"Which method of increasing my income does my subconscious self resonate with most?"*

- Write down **three or four potential ideas** on separate pieces of paper.

- Place them in front of you and hold the pendulum over each one.

- Observe which option generates **the strongest, most consistent movement**—this reveals the subconscious self's preference.

This technique **removes conscious bias** and allows the subconscious self to reveal its natural inclinations.

3. Strengthening Communication Through Writing (Subconscious Journaling)

Since the subconscious self does not think in **words** but in **images, emotions, and sensations**, one of the best ways to communicate is through **automatic writing or subconscious journaling**.

✅ **How to Practice Subconscious Journaling:**
1 **Start with a simple question:**

- *"What does my subconscious self want me to know today?"*

- *"What subconscious block am I ready to release?"*
  2 **Write freely without filtering.**
  3 **Look for recurring themes, phrases, or imagery.**
  4 **Over time, your subconscious responses will become clearer and more direct.**

By combining **pendulum work with subconscious journaling,** you create **a feedback loop** that strengthens the **depth and clarity of your communication.**

Using Rewards and Reinforcement to Encourage Cooperation
The subconscious self, much like a highly intelligent child, responds **extremely well to positive reinforcement.**

If you **acknowledge and reward** its cooperation, it will be **eager to continue helping.**

◈ **Praise Successful Responses**

- After a correct or helpful response, say: *"Thank you, subconscious self, for guiding me. I appreciate your help."*

- This acknowledgment **strengthens the relationship** and reinforces its willingness to participate.

◈ **Use a Physical Reward System**

- After **a successful subconscious training session,** engage in **a simple pleasurable activity** (e.g., a short walk, deep breath, or drinking a glass of water with intention).

- This **associates subconscious training with a positive outcome,** encouraging continued cooperation.

◈ **Celebrate Milestones**

- If the subconscious self has successfully helped clear an emotional block, recognize it:

  - *"We just released an old belief! Thank you for working with me on this!"*

Over time, **the subconscious self will respond faster and more effectively,** knowing that its efforts are appreciated.

Handling Resistance or Non-Cooperation

Occasionally, the subconscious self **may resist communication or training**. This can happen if:

✗ It still holds **deep-seated fears or protective mechanisms** from past experiences.

✗ It has been **ignored, criticized, or suppressed** for years.

✗ There are **hidden emotional blocks** preventing full cooperation.

If this happens, the most **direct and powerful solution** is to use the **Personal Demon Demolisher**, a structured energy-based process designed to **clear subconscious resistance and emotional blocks at their root**.

The **Personal Demon Demolisher** is an MSM technique that combines:

✓ **Energy psychology** – Releasing stored emotional imprints.
✓ **Neurovascular point activation** – Restoring flow between the subconscious and conscious self.
✓ **EFT-based clearing** – Disrupting and dissolving subconscious resistance.

Using the Personal Demon Demolisher to Clear Resistance

1 Identify the Block

- Use the **Pendulum Exercise** or journaling to uncover the **specific fear, resistance, or belief causing the issue**.

2 Engage the Personal Demon Demolisher Process

- Hold the **main frontal neurovascular points** (lightly placing your fingertips on your forehead).

- Bring the **resisted thought, fear, or block** into awareness.

- Use specific **tapping or pressure point activation** to **clear the emotional charge from the subconscious self**.

3 Reinforce the New Alignment

- After the clearing, **affirm the new subconscious alignment** with a statement such as:
  "My subconscious self fully supports my highest good and works in perfect harmony with my conscious self."

By using the **Personal Demon Demolisher**, subconscious blocks are not just **acknowledged**—they are **neutralized**, allowing for **full cooperation** between the subconscious self and the conscious self.

Unlike traditional affirmation-based methods that **try to override resistance**, this technique works **at the energetic level**, ensuring that resistance is **fully dissolved** rather than temporarily suppressed.

With this approach, the subconscious self moves from **hesitant and reactive** to **fully engaged and proactive in the manifestation process.**

Preparing for Advanced Subconscious Communication
Now that you have learned how to **expand, refine, and strengthen** communication, the next step is to introduce **advanced subconscious training techniques** that will:
✔ **Enhance intuition and energy perception.**
✔ **Increase the subconscious self's ability to influence reality.**
✔ **Fine-tune subconscious responses for even greater accuracy.**

In the next section, we will explore **advanced exercises** to develop the subconscious self into a **fully conscious, fully cooperative partner in manifestation.**

Because once your subconscious self is **trained to its highest potential**, you will no longer need to rely on external guidance—**your inner system will become your most powerful source of wisdom.**

Key Takeaways from This Section
💡 **The subconscious self's communication can be expanded**

beyond simple yes/no answers.

💡 **Percentage-based responses and subconscious journaling create deeper insights.**

💡 **Positive reinforcement encourages faster and more cooperative responses.**

💡 **Resistance can be fully cleared using the Personal Demon Demolisher.**

💡 **A trained subconscious self provides rapid, intuitive decision-making without overthinking.**

When the subconscious self becomes **a fully conscious co-creator**, manifestation becomes **effortless, natural, and precise**.

Section 12 – Strengthening the Subconscious Self for Advanced Manifestation

By this point, you have developed **direct communication with your subconscious self**, refined its responsiveness through **structured exercises**, and cleared resistance using **the Personal Demon Demolisher**.

Now, it's time to **take subconscious training to the next level**.

This phase focuses on **strengthening the subconscious self's ability to direct energy, hold powerful thought-forms, and enhance intuition**, making manifestation more **precise, efficient, and effortless**.

Most people rely **solely on willpower and conscious visualization**, but *Master the Science of Miracles®* teaches that **true manifestation happens when the subconscious self actively participates in the process**.

For this to happen, the subconscious self must:
✓ **Hold a stronger charge of vital life force energy.**
✓ **Refine its ability to sustain high-vibration thought-forms.**

✓ Increase its accuracy in detecting alignment and intuitive insights.

Expanding the Subconscious Self's Role in Energy Control

One of the subconscious self's **primary functions** is to **gather, store, and distribute** vital life force energy.

When properly trained, the subconscious self can:
✓ **Generate an excess charge of energy to fuel thought-forms.**
✓ **Direct energy to heal emotional, mental, and physical imbalances.**
✓ **Refine its ability to sustain high-frequency emotions like joy, gratitude, and love.**

If the subconscious self is **weak, scattered, or untrained**, manifestation becomes **slow and inconsistent**—because the thought-forms lack **enough energy to reach the Transcendent Self.**

To strengthen the subconscious self's ability to **hold and direct energy**, MSM includes specific **subconscious energy exercises.**

Subconscious Energy Strengthening Exercise: Lower Dan Tian Charge

The **Lower Dan Tian** is the body's **primary energy reservoir**, located just below the navel. In MSM, this is where the subconscious self **stores and accumulates vital life force energy.**

A **strong Lower Dan Tian** means the subconscious self can:
✓ **Hold a greater charge of energy, amplifying manifestation power.**
✓ **Maintain emotional stability and mental clarity.**
✓ **Project energy outward with precision and intention.**

How to Strengthen the Lower Dan Tian

1 **Place your hands over the Lower Dan Tian** (just below the navel).
2 **Breathe deeply and slowly, imagining energy gathering in this area.**
3 **As you inhale, mentally affirm:**

- *"My subconscious self strengthens its energy reserves."*
  ⬜As you exhale, feel the energy condense and grow denser.
  ⬜Repeat for 3-5 minutes daily.

Over time, this practice **trains the subconscious self to store an excess charge of energy**, ensuring that manifestations are powered by **strong, stable energy flow**.

Training the Subconscious Self to Strengthen Thought-Forms
Now that the subconscious self is **holding more energy**, the next step is to **train it to sustain high-vibration thought-forms over time**.

✓ **A weak subconscious self allows thought-forms to fade or dissipate.**
✓ **A trained subconscious self keeps thought-forms stable, powerful, and charged with energy.**

In *Chapter 3*, you learned how to create a **multi-sensory mental video**, the most effective way to structure and sustain an intention. This **mental video** allows your subconscious self to:
✓ **Accept the desired reality as already existing.**
✓ **Hold the thought-form with rich sensory detail.**
✓ **Amplify the energy behind the thought-form, making manifestation more effective.**

Now, you will train the subconscious self to **sustain the mental video with unwavering focus**—ensuring that it remains charged with energy and emotion until it manifests.

Thought-Form Strengthening Exercise
1 **Close your eyes and bring to mind the mental video you created in Chapter 3.**

- Replay it in vivid detail, activating all sensory elements.

- See it, hear it, and feel it as if it is already happening.

2 **Direct your subconscious self to hold the image steady.**

- As you focus on the mental video, affirm:
  "I am now sustaining this thought-form with unwavering, laser-like focus."

- Feel a deep sense of commitment to keeping the image alive and vibrant.

3 **Maintain the thought-form for as long as possible.**

- If it starts to fade, **re-engage it by amplifying sensory details.**

- Strengthen the emotional charge by feeling **gratitude, joy, and excitement** as though the manifestation is unfolding right now.

This exercise **trains the subconscious self to become the guardian of thought-forms**, ensuring that **your intentions remain energized and undisturbed.**

Enhancing Subconscious Sensitivity for Intuitive Guidance
As the subconscious self **gains strength**, it also becomes more **sensitive to energetic and intuitive information.**

Most people **ignore their subconscious signals** because they expect intuition to arrive as a **loud, undeniable voice**—but in reality, subconscious insights often come as:
✓ **A subtle gut feeling.**
✓ **A quiet knowing.**
✓ **An inner nudge toward the right action.**

To develop **subconscious intuition**, you must **train it to detect and amplify subtle insights.**

Subconscious Intuition Expansion Exercise
1 **Before making a decision, ask your subconscious self for guidance.**

- Example: *"Is this path aligned with my highest good?"*
  2 Sit quietly and pay attention to any physical sensations, emotions, or images that arise.
  3 If the sensation is expansive, warm, or light, it indicates alignment.
  4 If the sensation is heavy, constricted, or tight, it signals resistance.

This exercise **trains the subconscious self to communicate intuitive insights more clearly**, allowing you to navigate decisions **with greater ease and precision.**

The Final Phase of Subconscious Training
At this point, your subconscious self has been:
✓ **Cleared of major resistance using the Personal Demon Demolisher.**
✓ **Strengthened in its ability to hold and direct energy.**
✓ **Trained to sustain thought-forms for longer durations.**
✓ **Refined in its ability to provide intuitive insights.**

The final phase of subconscious training is **teaching it to project energy outward**, allowing you to:
✓ **Influence external reality with greater impact.**
✓ **Extend the reach of your thought-forms beyond your personal energy field.**
✓ **Strengthen your ability to interact with the energetic fabric of reality.**

In the next section, we will explore **advanced subconscious projection techniques**, which will allow you to **broadcast high-powered thought-forms into the quantum field for rapid manifestation.**

111

Because once the subconscious self is fully trained, **miracles don't just happen occasionally—they happen predictably, powerfully, and at will.**

Key Takeaways from This Section

💡 **The subconscious self must be trained to store and direct excess life force energy.**

💡 **A strong Lower Dan Tian enhances energy reserves, increasing manifestation power.**

💡 **The subconscious self must be trained to sustain thought-forms with unwavering focus.**

💡 **The mental video process (from Chapter 3) is the best tool for structuring and energizing manifestations.**

💡 **The next phase of training will focus on energy projection for external influence.**

When the subconscious self reaches its **full potential**, you step into **mastery of the unseen forces that shape reality.**

Section 13 – Training the Subconscious Self to Project Energy and Thought-Forms

Now that you have trained your subconscious self to **hold an excess charge of energy, sustain thought-forms, and refine intuitive perception**, the final phase of subconscious training is **energy projection**—the ability to direct energy outward to influence reality.

In *Master the Science of Miracles®*, energy projection is the key to:
✓ **Amplifying and transmitting thought-forms into the quantum field.**
✓ **Influencing physical reality with intention.**
✓ **Establishing a stronger connection with the Transcendent Self.**

Just as a **radio transmitter must send a strong signal for a station to be heard clearly**, your subconscious self must be trained to **send** out high-powered thought-forms so they can be received by the **Transcendent Self and reflected into your reality.**

This is where manifestation shifts from being an **internal process** to an **external force that reshapes the world around you.**

Why Energy Projection is Critical for Manifestation

Many people struggle with manifestation because their thought-forms **never leave their personal energy field.**

✓ If a thought-form is **weak or lacks energy**, it remains trapped within the subconscious self.
✓ If the subconscious self is **not trained to project energy outward**, the thought-form never reaches the Transcendent Self.
✓ If subconscious resistance exists, the thought-form is **blocked before it can fully transmit.**

For a manifestation to take hold in **external reality**, the subconscious self must be trained to **send out the thought-form with power, precision, and clarity.**

This is where **projection training** comes in.

The Energy Projection Exercise

This exercise strengthens the subconscious self's ability to **move energy outward**, ensuring that thought-forms are **delivered to the Transcendent Self effectively.**

Step 1: Activate the Mental Video

1 **Close your eyes and recall the mental video you created in Chapter 3.**
2 **Recreate it with full sensory immersion—seeing, hearing, and feeling the experience as real.**
3 **Engage deep, rhythmic breathing to increase energy flow.**

Step 2: Charge the Thought-Form with High-Energy Emotion

1 **Focus on the emotions that would arise if the mental video were already reality.**

- Feel **gratitude, joy, excitement, and certainty.**
  ⮀Amplify the energy by directing your breath toward the heart.

- The heart acts as a **step-up transformer**, increasing the energy of the thought-form.

Step 3: Project the Thought-Form Outward

1 **Imagine the thought-form as a sphere of energy in front of you.**
2 **Visualize it filling with light and power, expanding in intensity.**
3 **With your breath and intention, project the sphere outward.**

- *As you exhale, feel the thought-form move beyond your energy field, flowing into the universe.*

- *See it traveling on a wave of energy toward the Transcendent Self.*

4 **Affirm with certainty:**

- *"I now send this thought-form into the universe, fully energized and received by the Transcendent Self."*

- Feel a deep **sense of completion**, as though the process is already unfolding.

Training the Subconscious Self for Precision Projection
Energy projection is like learning to **throw a spear**—it requires **accuracy, power, and follow-through**.

To strengthen precision:
✓ **Practice sending thought-forms at different distances.**

- First, visualize sending them just outside your body.

- Then, project them further into a room.

- Eventually, expand to sending them beyond time and space.

✓ **Use focused breathing to enhance projection strength.**

- The **inhale gathers energy**, and the **exhale releases and directs it.**

✓ **Maintain a strong emotional charge during projection.**

- Emotion is the **carrier wave** that allows thought-forms to travel efficiently.

The more the subconscious self practices **intentional energy projection**, the more precise, powerful, and immediate your manifestations will become.

Strengthening the Connection Between the Subconscious and Transcendent Self

Energy projection is not just about **sending out desires**—it is also about **creating an open, two-way channel between the subconscious self and the Transcendent Self**.

Once the subconscious self learns to **transmit thought-forms**, it also becomes more **sensitive to receiving guidance and synchronicities from the Transcendent Self**.

✓ **After projection exercises, pay attention to subtle signs, inspirations, and intuitive nudges.**
✓ **Trust that the Transcendent Self is responding in real-time, orchestrating events in your favor.**
✓ **Maintain an open, receptive state by practicing deep listening and heightened awareness.**

Over time, the subconscious self will:
✓ **Recognize and act on divine guidance with greater ease.**
✓ **Strengthen its ability to align with the universal flow of miracles.**

✓ Become a clear, open channel for receiving insights and manifestations.

The Final Integration: Becoming a Master of Your Subconscious Self
At this point, you have:
✓ Developed clear, direct communication with your subconscious self.
✓ Trained it to sustain high-energy thought-forms through the mental video process.
✓ Cleared subconscious resistance using the Personal Demon Demolisher.
✓ Strengthened its ability to project thought-forms outward with power and precision.
✓ Opened the subconscious self to receive guidance and synchronicities from the Transcendent Self.

Now, you are no longer merely "practicing" manifestation.

You are now operating as a **Master of the Science of Miracles®—** where thoughts, energy, and reality move **in harmony with your intention.**

Final Reflection: The Role of the Subconscious Self in Miracles
Your subconscious self is not just a **passive part of you**—it is the **bridge between the physical world and the Transcendent Self.**

✓ It **manages your energy.**
✓ It **holds and sustains your thought-forms.**
✓ It **projects those thought-forms into reality.**
✓ It **receives divine guidance and orchestrates synchronicities.**

When trained, the subconscious self becomes **the greatest ally in your spiritual and manifestation journey**—allowing you to move beyond struggle, doubt, and resistance into a **life of certainty, power, and effortless miracles.**

Key Takeaways from This Section
♀ **Energy projection is the key to making thought-forms take hold in external reality.**
♀ **A trained subconscious self can project energy outward with power, clarity, and precision.**
♀ **The mental video process (from Chapter 3) serves as the structured foundation for projection.**
♀ **The subconscious self must be strengthened through repeated projection exercises.**
♀ **Once trained, the subconscious self becomes a direct channel between you and the Transcendent Self.**

When you reach this level of subconscious mastery, **manifestation is no longer a question of "if"—it is a matter of certainty.**

What Comes Next?
This chapter has taken you through the **entire process of training the subconscious self**—from basic awareness to full manifestation power.

Now, in the next chapter, we will explore how to **synchronize all three aspects of the human being—the conscious self, the subconscious self, and the Transcendent Self**—so they work as a **unified force**, amplifying your power to create **miracles on demand.**

Because when all three selves are aligned, **miracles don't just happen occasionally—they become your way of life.**

Chapter 5: Developing the Hidden Skills of the Subconscious Self

Section 1 – Introduction: The Hidden Talents of the Subconscious Self

The **subconscious self** is often thought of as a passive storehouse of memories, emotions, and autonomic functions. But in reality, it possesses **unique, hidden abilities** that are essential for manifestation, energy transmission, and direct interaction with the Transcendent Self.

These abilities remain dormant in most people because they have never been trained to recognize or develop them. Yet, they are just as natural as memory, intuition, and emotion—when properly cultivated, they allow you to:
✓ **Perceive energies beyond the range of the five physical senses.**
✓ **Form energetic connections with people, places, and objects across space and time.**
✓ **Send and receive thought-forms with precision and accuracy.**

Without these skills, the subconscious self operates at a **basic level**, responding only to past programming and emotional conditioning. But once trained, it becomes a **highly refined instrument for gathering information, transmitting energy, and manifesting desires into reality.**

This chapter will focus on developing the **three primary skills of the subconscious self** that are essential for working with *Master the Science of Miracles®*:

The Three Hidden Skills of the Subconscious Self
1 **Sensing Energies Beyond the Physical World**

- The subconscious self has the ability to detect and interact with **subtle energy fields** from minerals, plants, animals, and people.

- This allows for **a deeper understanding of the unseen forces that shape reality.**

2 **Attaching Energetic Threads to People, Places, and Objects**

- The subconscious self naturally **forms fine, invisible threads** (sometimes called etheric cords) that connect it to everything it interacts with.

- These **threads remain active even after time and distance separate you from the object or person.**

3 **Sending and Receiving Thought-Forms Through These Threads**

- These energetic connections allow for **the transmission of thought-forms, impressions, and even emotions** from one subconscious self to another.

- Thought-forms do not remain confined to the mind; they travel along these **energetic pathways** to influence reality.

Why These Abilities Are Essential for Manifestation
Many people struggle with manifestation because they are **only using their conscious self**—they form an intention and visualize an outcome, but the **subconscious self is untrained in transmitting that desire to the Transcendent Self**.

✓ The **Transcendent Self does not perceive physical reality directly**—it relies on the subconscious self to send it information.
✓ If the subconscious self **lacks energy or focus**, the thought-form will be **weak and ineffective.**
✓ If the subconscious self **has not been trained to project thought-forms outward**, the manifestation remains **stagnant** instead of taking shape in external reality.

This is why mastering these subconscious abilities is not just **helpful**—it is **essential** for deliberate manifestation.

Activating the Subconscious Self as a Co-Creator
The conscious self alone **cannot manifest physical changes**—it must work **in harmony with the subconscious self** to:

119

✓ Generate, store, and direct energy toward an intention.

✓ Transmit thought-forms with precision.

✓ Ensure the Transcendent Self receives and responds to the request.

In this chapter, you will begin **awakening the latent abilities of your subconscious self**, training it to:

✓ **Expand beyond its basic functions and into mastery of energy transmission.**

✓ **Strengthen its ability to attach, retrieve, and send thought-forms along etheric threads.**

✓ **Develop the capacity to perceive and influence reality in ways most people never access.**

Once these skills are developed, **you will no longer struggle with the process of manifestation**—because your subconscious self will be **actively working with you, rather than passively following old patterns.**

The next section will explore **the essential role of these subconscious skills in manifestation**, providing a deeper understanding of how the subconscious self serves as the **bridge between thought and physical reality.**

Key Takeaways from This Section

💡 The subconscious self is **not just a reactive mind—it possesses unique abilities essential for manifestation.**

💡 These hidden skills include **sensing energy, forming energetic threads, and transmitting thought-forms.**

💡 Most people fail at manifestation because their subconscious self **is untrained in transmitting their desires to the Transcendent Self.**

💡 This chapter will train the subconscious self to **become an active, powerful co-creator in the manifestation process.**

Section 2 – The Essential Role of These Skills in Manifestation

The **subconscious self is the bridge between thought and physical reality**—it is the conduit through which desires are transmitted to the Transcendent Self. Without its participation, manifestation remains **fragmented, inconsistent, or entirely ineffective.**

Most people struggle with manifestation **not because they lack desire or clarity,** but because their subconscious self has **not been trained to properly send and receive thought-forms.**

In *Master the Science of Miracles®*, true manifestation occurs when the subconscious self:
✓ **Generates and holds an excess charge of energy.**
✓ **Forms strong, stable connections to people, places, and outcomes.**
✓ **Transmits thought-forms along etheric threads to the Transcendent Self.**

When the subconscious self is untrained, **manifestation feels like a guessing game.**
When it is trained, **manifestation becomes a structured, reliable process.**

Why the Subconscious Self is Critical for Manifestation
The conscious self may have the **desire to manifest**, but it lacks the ability to **direct energy and project thought-forms.** That responsibility belongs to the **subconscious self.**

✓ The **conscious self sets the intention**—it decides what is to be created.
✓ The **subconscious self builds the thought-form**—it gathers energy, attaches emotion, and transmits it outward.
✓ The **Transcendent Self receives the thought-form** and **reshapes external reality** accordingly.

If the subconscious self is **weak, scattered, or distracted**, the thought-form never reaches the Transcendent Self with enough clarity or force to take effect. This is why:
✓ **Scattered thoughts lead to scattered results.**
✓ **Low energy levels lead to weak manifestations.**
✓ **Conflicting emotions can override the intended thought-form.**

When properly trained, the subconscious self becomes **a direct transmission channel between desire and reality.**

How the Subconscious Self Transmits Thought-Forms
The subconscious self does not communicate through **words or logic**—it communicates through **images, emotions, and energy.**

To send a thought-form to the Transcendent Self, the subconscious self must:
1 **Form a clear, multi-sensory mental video of the desired outcome.**
2 **Charge the thought-form with high-vibration emotions.**
3 **Project the thought-form outward through subconscious etheric threads.**
4 **Release the thought-form with certainty, trusting that it has been received.**

Each of these steps requires **specific subconscious skills**, which will be developed in this chapter.

The Three Most Common Manifestation Mistakes
People who struggle with manifestation **often make one or more of the following subconscious errors:**

Mistake #1: Trying to Manifest with the Conscious Mind Alone

✓ Many people believe that **if they just think about something long enough, it will manifest.**
✓ But the conscious self **cannot** manifest directly—it must send

thought-forms through the **subconscious self.**

✓ Without subconscious training, **manifestation efforts feel like "wishing" rather than a deliberate process.**

✅ **The Solution:** Strengthen the subconscious self's ability to project thought-forms outward with precision and energy.

Mistake #2: Sending Weak or Contradictory Thought-Forms

✓ If the subconscious self sends a **poorly-formed** thought, it will **not be received effectively.**

✓ If the subconscious self sends **two opposing thought-forms** (e.g., wanting success but fearing visibility), they **cancel each other out.**

✅ **The Solution:** Train the subconscious self to **generate stable, single-focus thought-forms charged with positive emotion.**

Mistake #3: Failing to Build an Excess Charge of Energy

✓ The subconscious self requires **an excess charge of energy** to effectively transmit thought-forms.

✓ If a person is **drained, stressed, or fearful**, their subconscious self lacks the power to **send out a strong transmission.**

✅ **The Solution:** Strengthen the subconscious self's **Lower Dan Tian energy reserves** and reinforce its ability to **hold and direct energy.**

Training the Subconscious Self for Manifestation Success
Developing the subconscious self's abilities allows for **precise, deliberate manifestation** rather than hit-or-miss results.

In this chapter, you will:
✓ **Train the subconscious self to sense and collect energy more effectively.**
✓ **Develop the ability to form etheric threads that maintain strong**

connections.
✓ **Practice transmitting thought-forms with clarity and power.**

By the end of this training, your subconscious self will **no longer act as an untrained force working against you**—it will become **a fully developed partner in creating miracles.**

The next section will explore **how the subconscious self forms etheric threads** and how these connections can be strengthened for precise manifestation.

Key Takeaways from This Section
💡 **The subconscious self is the essential bridge between the conscious self and the Transcendent Self.**
💡 **Manifestation fails when the subconscious self is untrained in energy projection.**
💡 **The subconscious self does not use words—it transmits thought-forms through images, emotions, and energy.**
💡 **Training the subconscious self eliminates weak, scattered, or contradictory manifestations.**
💡 **The next section will focus on subconscious etheric threads and their role in transmitting energy.**

Section 3 – Subconscious Threads and Their Function

At this stage, you understand that the subconscious self plays an essential role in **manifestation**—serving as the bridge between the conscious self and the Transcendent Self. But how exactly does it send and receive thought-forms?

The answer lies in **subconscious etheric threads**—the invisible energetic connections that link your subconscious self to people, places, objects, and events.

These **subconscious threads** are always forming, strengthening, and dissolving throughout your daily life. With proper training, you can **intentionally direct them** to enhance **manifestation, intuition, and energetic influence.**

What Are Subconscious Etheric Threads?
Whenever you **touch, see, hear, or think intently about something,** your subconscious self automatically forms an **energetic thread** that connects you to that object, place, or person.

✓ If you think about a friend you haven't spoken to in years, your subconscious self **re-establishes the thread** that once connected you.
✓ If you enter a room and suddenly feel uneasy, your subconscious self is **picking up impressions through threads** attached to the space.
✓ If you hold an object that belonged to someone else, you may sense emotions or memories linked to it—this is because the object still holds **an active subconscious thread from its previous owner.**

These threads are **not physical**—they exist in the **etheric substance** of the subconscious self. They function like **energetic pathways,** allowing for:
✓ **The transmission of thought-forms.**
✓ **The reception of impressions from distant objects or people.**
✓ **The reinforcement of connections between you and your desired manifestations.**

How Subconscious Threads Form and Function
◈ **Threads Are Naturally Created Through Interaction**

- Anytime you focus your attention on something—whether physically or mentally—a subconscious thread **forms automatically.**

- The more attention or emotion you attach to something, the **stronger the thread becomes.**

◈ Threads Can Be Strengthened or Weakened

- A thread grows **stronger** with repeated interaction, emotional energy, or deliberate focus.

- A thread **weakens over time** if no energy is sent along it, eventually dissolving.

◈ Threads Transmit Thought-Forms and Energy

- The subconscious self can **send energy, emotion, or intention through these threads.**

- This allows for **intuitive insights, energetic influence, and manifestation precision.**

These subconscious threads explain many everyday experiences that most people dismiss as coincidence. For example:

✓ Have you ever thought about someone, only for them to suddenly call you?

✓ Have you ever walked into a room and immediately sensed tension, joy, or sadness?

✓ Have you ever picked up an old object and felt memories or emotions linked to it?

All of these experiences result from **subconscious threads transmitting information.**

Harnessing Subconscious Threads for Manifestation

To **consciously** use subconscious threads for manifestation, you must train the subconscious self to:

✓ **Intentionally form and strengthen specific threads.**

✓ **Directly send energy, emotion, and thought-forms through them.**

✓ **Retrieve impressions from distant objects or people.**

Without this training, your subconscious self will continue forming and dissolving threads **randomly**, rather than in a way that supports your manifestations.

By **directing these threads toward a desired outcome**, you create an **active connection between yourself and your goal**, ensuring that energy continuously flows toward manifestation.

Practical Training: Strengthening Subconscious Threads

To gain control over subconscious threads, you must first learn how to **intentionally form and reinforce them.**

Try this simple **Subconscious Thread Reinforcement Exercise**:

Step 1: Select a Target

Choose an object, place, or person you want to strengthen a subconscious connection with.

Step 2: Activate the Connection

✔ **Hold the object (if possible) or look at a picture of the place/person.**
✔ **Close your eyes and visualize a fine thread extending from your subconscious self to the target.**
✔ **Feel the thread connecting, growing stronger with each breath.**

Step 3: Reinforce the Thread with Emotion

✔ Send a **specific feeling or intention** down the thread—gratitude, love, certainty.
✔ If manifesting an outcome, visualize it **already happening** and flowing toward you.
✔ Imagine the energy traveling smoothly, ensuring the connection remains strong.

Step 4: Check for Impressions

✓ Once the thread is formed, remain still and listen.
✓ See if you receive **any emotions, sensations, or images related to the target.**
✓ This is your subconscious self **sending information back to you.**

This practice **strengthens the subconscious self's ability to form stable, intentional connections,** making manifestation **more direct and precise.**

How Subconscious Threads Influence Others
Subconscious threads **don't just transmit energy—they can also influence the subconscious selves of others.**

✓ When you **think about someone with strong emotion,** your subconscious self **sends an energetic signal** along the thread.
✓ This is why **people often feel compelled to call, text, or think about you when you strongly focus on them.**
✓ It also explains why **repeated thought about a person strengthens their presence in your life.**

This is not manipulation—it is the **natural function of subconscious threads.**
When used ethically, it allows for:
✓ **Strengthened relationships and deeper connections.**
✓ **A heightened ability to attract supportive people into your life.**
✓ **Sending positive, healing energy to others from a distance.**

Subconscious Threads and Non-Local Impressions
Non-local communication is simply **the subconscious self using etheric threads to send and receive impressions.**

✓ When you **send a mental message to someone,** their subconscious self **receives it along the thread**—whether they consciously recognize it or not.
✓ If the recipient is sensitive, they may **suddenly think of you, dream**

about you, or feel an unexplained urge to contact you.
✓ This happens because **the subconscious self operates beyond time and space**, allowing for near-instantaneous transmission of impressions.

Training in this ability allows for:
✓ **More precise communication with others at a subconscious level.**
✓ **Heightened intuitive perception—knowing what someone is thinking or feeling before they express it.**
✓ **Strengthened manifestation, as thought-forms can be transmitted more efficiently.**

The Next Step: Using Subconscious Threads for Remote Perception
Now that you understand **how subconscious threads form and function**, the next section will explore **how to use them to retrieve information from distant people, places, and objects.**

By refining this ability, you will:
✓ **Gain insight into people and events without physical interaction.**
✓ **Expand your ability to "see" beyond what the physical senses perceive.**
✓ **Train the subconscious self to actively retrieve data rather than passively absorb it.**

This is a crucial step toward **mastering the hidden skills of the subconscious self** and **enhancing your ability to influence reality.**

Key Takeaways from This Section
💡 Subconscious threads are energetic connections between your subconscious self and everything you interact with.
💡 These threads allow for the transmission of energy, thought-forms, and intuitive impressions.

💡 Manifestation becomes more effective when you intentionally strengthen threads to your desired outcome.

💡 Threads also influence others, creating subconscious communication pathways.

💡 In the next section, you will learn how to use these threads for remote perception and information retrieval.

Section 4 – Developing Sensory Projection Skills

Now that you understand how the subconscious self forms and maintains **subconscious threads**, the next step is learning how to use these threads for **sensory projection**—the ability to retrieve impressions from distant people, places, and objects.

Sensory projection is **not the same as physical sight, hearing, or touch**—it is the subconscious self's ability to **send awareness through etheric threads** and receive information beyond the physical senses.

This ability explains why you can sometimes:
✓ **Think of a person and suddenly "feel" their mood, even before speaking to them.**
✓ **Walk into a room and instantly sense the emotional atmosphere.**
✓ **Hold an object and get a mental image or feeling about its history.**

The subconscious self is constantly gathering **sensory impressions** through its threads—it is simply a matter of **training yourself to recognize and interpret them.**

How Sensory Projection Works

Sensory projection follows a **three-step process:**

1 **The subconscious self forms an etheric thread to a person, object, or place.**

- This happens automatically when you focus your attention on something.

2 Your subconscious self sends a small "extension" of awareness down the thread.

- This is like casting out a **fishing line**—you are sending out your perception to connect with the target.

3 The subconscious self retrieves an impression and sends it back to the conscious self.

- The impression arrives as **an image, feeling, or subtle knowing.**
- Many people dismiss these impressions as imagination, not realizing they are real data.

By training yourself to **trust and interpret these impressions**, you will **expand your perception beyond the limits of the five physical senses.**

The Common Challenge: Discerning Real Impressions from Imagination

The biggest obstacle in developing sensory projection is **learning to distinguish real impressions from random thoughts.**

✓ The subconscious self does **not communicate in full sentences or direct words**—it sends **symbols, emotions, and images** instead.
✓ The information is often **subtle and easy to overlook** unless you are trained to recognize it.
✓ Many people **immediately dismiss their first impressions as "just their imagination,"** blocking their ability to perceive correctly.

The key to developing accuracy is to treat every impression as important, even if it feels vague at first. With practice, the subconscious self will refine its ability to send clearer, more reliable impressions.

Training Exercise: Projecting Sensory Awareness to an Object
This exercise strengthens the subconscious self's ability to **extend awareness through a subconscious thread and retrieve impressions.**

Step 1: Select an Object You Are Unfamiliar With

✓ Have someone place a **small object inside a box or envelope** so you cannot see it.
✓ The object should have been handled frequently (like a ring, key, or tool), so it carries **strong subconscious threads from its owner.**

Step 2: Extend Awareness to the Object

✓ Place your hand **just above the box/envelope** without opening it.
✓ Close your eyes and focus on **feeling a subtle connection** forming between your subconscious self and the object.
✓ Imagine an **etheric thread extending from your solar plexus to the object.**

Step 3: Retrieve the First Impression

✓ Allow the subconscious self to **send back an image, feeling, or sense related to the object.**
✓ Do not analyze—simply note whatever appears, even if it seems random.
✓ Ask yourself:

- Does the object feel **light or heavy**?

- Does it feel **warm, cold, metallic, soft**?

- Do any **memories, emotions, or images** come up?

Step 4: Verify the Impressions

✓ Open the box and examine the object.
✓ Compare your impressions with the actual characteristics of the

object.
✓ Repeat the exercise daily—accuracy will improve over time.

Advancing to Remote Sensory Projection
Once you have trained the subconscious self to perceive impressions
from **nearby objects**, you can advance to projecting awareness to
distant locations.

This skill allows you to:
✓ **Tune into the energy of a location before visiting.**
✓ **Sense the emotional state of a loved one before talking to them.**
✓ **Perceive hidden information about places, objects, or people.**

The process is the same as the **object projection exercise**—but
instead of focusing on an object, you will focus on a **place or person**
that is not physically present.

Training Exercise: Remote Perception of a Location

1 **Choose a location you are familiar with but not currently in.**

- This could be a friend's house, a park, or a favorite store.

2 **Close your eyes and visualize a thread connecting you to that
place.**

- Imagine your subconscious self extending awareness along the
thread.

3 **Ask your subconscious self to send back impressions.**

- What is the **emotional atmosphere** of the place?

- Are there any **dominant colors, sounds, or sensations**?

- Do any **people, objects, or smells** come to mind?

4 **Write down your impressions before verifying them.**

- If possible, visit the location later and compare your perceptions with reality.

With practice, the subconscious self will **send back more detailed and precise impressions.**

Practical Applications of Sensory Projection
Training sensory projection allows for **a wide range of practical applications**:

✓ **Personal Safety** – Tune into locations before visiting to sense whether they feel safe or energetically chaotic.
✓ **Strengthened Intuition** – Gain instant subconscious awareness of people's emotions, intentions, and energy states.
✓ **Finding Lost Objects** – Attach an etheric thread to a missing item and let the subconscious self send back an impression of its location.

✓ **Manifestation Precision** – By projecting sensory awareness into a **future reality where your manifestation is already fulfilled**, you engage the **principle of quantum superposition**—where multiple potential realities exist simultaneously.

In quantum physics, superposition states that **all possible outcomes exist at once until observation collapses them into a singular reality.**

☑ By **fully immersing yourself in the sensory experience of your future self**, you create the conditions that allow that reality to become **the one that collapses into existence.**
☑ The more **vivid, real, and emotionally charged** the projected experience is, the stronger the subconscious transmission.
☑ This is why the **mental video technique** from *Chapter 3* is so effective—it **anchors your awareness in the desired reality**, reinforcing the subconscious self's ability to **make it your present experience.**

Rather than simply *thinking* about what you want to manifest, **you are placing yourself inside the reality of it, collapsing the singularity in your favor.**

Preparing for the Next Level: Sending Thought-Forms Through Subconscious Threads

Now that you have trained the subconscious self to **retrieve information** through etheric threads, the next step is learning how to **send energy, emotions, and thought-forms** through these threads to influence reality.

✓ **Every thought and emotion carries an energetic signature** that can be sent along subconscious threads.
✓ **A properly formed thought-form can travel great distances and influence people, places, and circumstances.**
✓ **This is the key to conscious manifestation, as thought-forms must reach the Transcendent Self to be realized in physical form.**

The next section will explore **how to project thought-forms effectively, ensuring that they are received and acted upon by the Transcendent Self.**

Key Takeaways from This Section

💡 **Sensory projection is the subconscious self's ability to perceive beyond the five physical senses.**

💡 **Manifesting by projecting sensory awareness into your desired future reality collapses the singularity in your favor.**

💡 **The next section will cover how to use subconscious threads to send energy and thought-forms outward.**

Section 5 – The Role of the Alpha Brainwave State in Sending Thought-Forms

Now that you have trained the subconscious self to **retrieve information through subconscious threads**, the next step is learning how to **send energy, emotions, and thought-forms outward** to shape reality.

This process requires more than just **visualization**—it requires entering the **alpha brainwave state**, where the subconscious self becomes **highly receptive, fluid, and responsive to thought-forms.**

The **alpha state** is the ideal mental frequency for **transmitting manifestations,** because it:
✓ **Removes the barriers of past, present, and future**, allowing thought-forms to be experienced as present reality.
✓ **Reduces interference from the conscious mind**, making subconscious transmissions more effective.
✓ **Aligns the subconscious self with the Transcendent Self,** ensuring clear reception of thought-forms.

Mastering **thought-form projection in the alpha state** is what separates **casual wishful thinking from deliberate, repeatable manifestation.**

Why the Alpha State is Critical for Thought-Form Transmission
The **Transcendent Self does not perceive time the way the conscious self does**—it exists in a realm where all moments are simultaneous.

For a manifestation to take hold, the subconscious self must:
✓ **Form a multi-sensory thought-form as though it is happening now.**
✓ **Hold the thought-form long enough for the Transcendent Self to register it as real.**
✓ **Send the thought-form outward with an excess charge of energy.**

The **alpha state** is the key to **removing time-based resistance**—it allows the subconscious self to treat the thought-form **as if it is already reality**, ensuring a **clean, powerful transmission.**

If a person remains in a **high-beta state (analytical thinking, stress, doubt)** while trying to manifest, the subconscious self:
✘ **Struggles to send a clear signal to the Transcendent Self.**
✘ **Attaches contradictory emotions like doubt or fear to the thought-form.**
✘ **Prevents the thought-form from fully taking shape in reality.**

This is why **manifesting from a deep alpha state** is **far more effective** than simply "thinking positive thoughts" throughout the day.

How to Enter the Alpha State for Thought-Form Transmission
The **alpha state** occurs naturally when you are:
✔ Just about to fall asleep or wake up.
✔ In a relaxed, meditative state.
✔ Engaged in deep focus or creative visualization.

To **intentionally enter the alpha state for manifestation**, follow this process:

Step 1: Relax the Body and Mind

✔ Sit or lie down in a quiet space.
✔ Take deep, slow breaths, exhaling tension with each breath.
✔ Let your body feel **heavy and relaxed**.

Step 2: Use a Simple Mental Anchor

✔ Close your eyes and count backward from **10 to 1**, imagining each number pulling you deeper into relaxation.
✔ Alternatively, you can visualize yourself **descending a staircase** or **floating downward into a deep, peaceful state.**

Step 3: Activate the Thought-Form

137

✓ Recall the **multi-sensory mental video** from *Chapter 3*—experiencing it **as if it is happening now**.
✓ Engage all **five senses** to make the experience vivid.
✓ Feel the emotions of **gratitude, joy, and certainty** as though the manifestation is already real.

Step 4: Send the Thought-Form Outward

✓ Imagine the thought-form as a **sphere of energy** in front of you.
✓ See it **growing brighter and more intense** as you focus on it.
✓ With each exhale, visualize the thought-form moving **beyond your body, beyond the room, and into the universe.**
✓ Mentally affirm:

- *"This reality is already mine. It is unfolding perfectly."*

- *"I now release this thought-form to the Transcendent Self."*

Using the Alpha State to Strengthen Thought-Forms
A well-formed thought-form must be:
✓ **Held steady in the subconscious self long enough for transmission.**
✓ **Charged with high-energy emotions like joy and certainty.**
✓ **Released without attachment, allowing it to take root in reality.**

If a thought-form is created **without entering alpha**, it may lack:
✗ **Stability** – It fades before being fully transmitted.
✗ **Emotional power** – It lacks the energy to manifest.
✗ **Clarity** – The subconscious self may send mixed signals, weakening the request.

When **trained properly**, the subconscious self becomes **so proficient at sending thought-forms in the alpha state** that it eventually:
✓ **Does it automatically whenever an intention is formed.**
✓ **Begins responding to reality in real-time, adjusting projections as needed.**

✔ Transmits desires directly to the Transcendent Self without interference.

Quantum Manifestation: The Role of Alpha in Collapsing Potential Realities

As discussed in **Chapter 4**, quantum superposition states that **multiple potential realities exist simultaneously**—until an observer collapses one into existence.

The **alpha state enhances this effect** because:
✔ It places you in the **most receptive mental frequency** for **collapsing singularities in your favor**.
✔ It allows you to **fully embody the experience of the desired reality**, increasing its probability of manifestation.
✔ It ensures that **the subconscious self accepts the thought-form as present reality**, preventing self-sabotage.

Without alpha, the conscious mind remains **too rigidly attached to past experiences**, reinforcing the idea that "things are as they have always been."

With alpha, the subconscious self moves into **a fluid state of possibility**, making **new realities easier to access and integrate**.

This is why **all advanced manifestation techniques involve entering altered states**—they allow the subconscious self to **bridge the gap between what exists and what is being created.**

Training the Subconscious Self to Enter Alpha on Command

To strengthen **alpha-induced manifestation**, practice the following daily:

✔ **Morning and Evening Alpha Practice** – The moments right after waking and just before sleep are **naturally alpha-dominant**. Use these times to reinforce **mental videos and thought-forms.**
✔ **Breath and Relaxation Training** – Daily relaxation exercises make

it easier to enter alpha **on command.**
✓ **Consistent Visualization in Alpha** – The more often you practice **sending thought-forms from alpha**, the faster the subconscious self **integrates this skill into daily reality.**

The more you train in **alpha-based projection**, the more the subconscious self will **automatically operate at this frequency**, ensuring **continuous, precise manifestation.**

The Next Step: Projecting Thought-Forms Through Etheric Threads

Now that you understand **how the alpha state enhances manifestation**, the next section will explore **how to send thought-forms through subconscious threads**, ensuring that they reach the intended target with **maximum precision and power.**

✓ **A well-formed thought-form must not only be clear and emotionally charged—it must be sent to the right place.**
✓ **The subconscious self uses etheric threads to direct thought-forms to people, places, and the Transcendent Self.**
✓ **Mastering this technique ensures that your manifestations are not just "sent out," but actually received and acted upon.**

The next section will provide **structured training on how to project thought-forms through subconscious etheric threads**, allowing for **direct influence over reality.**

Key Takeaways from This Section

💡 **The alpha state is the ideal brainwave state for transmitting thought-forms.**

💡 **In alpha, the subconscious self is most receptive, fluid, and able to manifest without resistance.**

💡 **Quantum superposition works in alpha because it allows you to collapse the singularity in your favor.**

💡 Training the subconscious self to enter alpha on command increases manifestation speed and accuracy.

💡 The next section will cover how to send thought-forms through subconscious etheric threads.

Section 6 – Projecting Thought-Forms Through Etheric Threads

Now that you understand how the **alpha state enhances manifestation**, the next step is learning how to **direct thought-forms through subconscious etheric threads** to ensure they reach their intended target with **maximum precision and power**.

A well-formed thought-form **must not only be clear and emotionally charged**—it must also be **delivered accurately**. Without direction, thought-forms may:

✘ **Dissipate** before reaching their destination.

✘ **Remain trapped in the subconscious self** without being transmitted.

✘ **Be received by unintended recipients**, causing mixed or unexpected results.

By using **subconscious threads as energetic pathways**, the subconscious self ensures that **each thought-form is delivered with focus, accuracy, and influence**—whether to a person, a location, or the Transcendent Self.

How Thought-Forms Travel Through Subconscious Threads

As covered in **Section 3**, subconscious threads act as **etheric connections** between you and everything you interact with. These threads serve as **highways** for transmitting:

✓ **Sensory impressions** (retrieving information from a distance).

✓ **Emotional energy** (sending feelings or intentions to others).

✓ **Thought-forms** (projecting manifestations into reality).

141

When a thought-form is sent through a **strong, well-formed subconscious thread**, it:

✓ **Travels instantly to its destination, regardless of distance.**

✓ **Carries the emotional charge necessary to influence reality.**

✓ **Returns feedback from the recipient or target, providing intuitive confirmation.**

Without a directed thread, the thought-form may **lose focus or dissipate**, weakening its effectiveness.

Three Primary Targets for Thought-Form Projection

The subconscious self can direct thought-forms to three main destinations:

1 Sending Thought-Forms to Another Person

- This is used for **influencing relationships, sending healing energy, or strengthening connections.**

- Thought-forms travel along **pre-existing subconscious threads** that already link you to the person.

- The recipient may **sense the transmission consciously or unconsciously**, responding with action, emotion, or intuitive recognition.

✅ **Example:** If you want to reconnect with a distant friend, you can project a thought-form of **seeing yourself happily speaking with them**, attached to a **strong emotional charge of warmth and excitement.**

---

2 Sending Thought-Forms to a Future Event or Goal

- This is used for **manifestation, goal-setting, and aligning with a desired future.**

- The subconscious self projects the thought-form into **a future point in time** where the event has already occurred.

- The projection **anchors a strong connection** between present reality and the desired outcome, increasing the probability of its manifestation.

✅ **Example:** If you are preparing for an important business opportunity, you can project a thought-form of **your future self walking into the room with confidence, feeling successful, and achieving your goal.**

This technique engages **quantum superposition**, helping to **collapse the singularity in your favor**, as discussed in **Section 4**.

---

3 Sending Thought-Forms to the Transcendent Self

- This is the most **powerful form of thought-form projection**, used for **divine guidance, spiritual growth, and high-level manifestation.**

- The subconscious self must **convert the thought-form into a form that the Transcendent Self can recognize and respond to.**

- This requires **a deep alpha state, high emotional charge, and full surrender** to the process.

✅ **Example:** If you are seeking guidance on an important life decision, you can project a thought-form that expresses **your desired outcome, feelings of trust, and an openness to receive divine insight.**

Training Exercise: Thought-Form Projection Through Subconscious Threads

This exercise trains the subconscious self to **send thought-forms with precision and intention** through etheric threads.

Step 1: Select a Target for Your Thought-Form

Choose one of the three targets:
✓ **A person you wish to influence or reconnect with.**
✓ **A future event or goal you want to reinforce.**
✓ **The Transcendent Self for guidance or manifestation.**

Step 2: Enter the Alpha State

✓ Relax deeply, using **the alpha induction method from Section 5.**
✓ Ensure you are in a **calm, receptive, and focused state.**

Step 3: Create the Thought-Form

✓ Recall the **multi-sensory mental video** from *Chapter 3* that represents your intention.
✓ Engage **sight, sound, touch, emotion, and movement** to make it real.
✓ Charge the thought-form with **gratitude, certainty, and joy.**

Step 4: Attach the Thought-Form to a Subconscious Thread

✓ If sending to a **person**, visualize the thread connecting you to them, glowing with energy.
✓ If sending to a **future event**, see a thread extending **through time** toward that moment.
✓ If sending to the **Transcendent Self**, visualize the thread **stretching upward into an infinite, radiant light.**

Step 5: Project the Thought-Form Through the Thread

✓ Imagine the thought-form **traveling along the thread, moving effortlessly toward its destination.**
✓ Feel a **wave of energy flowing outward** as the transmission is sent.
✓ Affirm with confidence:

- *"This thought-form is now delivered with perfect clarity and power."*

- *"I release this thought-form and trust in its fulfillment."*

How to Know If a Thought-Form Was Successfully Sent

When a thought-form is projected correctly, you may experience:

✓ **A sudden lightness or sense of completion.**

✓ **An intuitive confirmation, such as a knowing or unexpected synchronicity.**

✓ **A response from the target (e.g., the person reaches out, the event unfolds smoothly, or guidance arrives unexpectedly).**

If no confirmation occurs, it may indicate:

✗ **The thought-form lacked emotional charge.**

✗ **The transmission was blocked by doubt or subconscious interference.**

✗ **The subconscious self did not hold the thought-form long enough before release.**

With practice, the subconscious self **becomes highly proficient** at sending thought-forms **with immediate, visible results.**

The Next Step: Strengthening Thought-Forms for Greater Influence

Now that you have learned how to **send thought-forms through subconscious threads**, the next section will explore **how to strengthen and reinforce thought-forms** so they:

✓ **Remain active longer.**

✓ **Influence reality more powerfully.**

✓ **Continue receiving energy even after transmission.**

Many people unknowingly **weaken their own manifestations** by:

✗ **Doubting their thought-forms after sending them.**

✗ **Attaching mixed emotions that distort the transmission.**

✗ **Failing to reinforce the thought-form with continued energy.**

The next section will introduce **advanced techniques for sustaining, amplifying, and reinforcing thought-forms**, ensuring that **they continue working long after they are sent.**

Key Takeaways from This Section

💡 Subconscious threads serve as the delivery system for sending thought-forms.

💡 Manifestations are more effective when thought-forms are sent through precise, intentional connections.

💡 Three primary targets exist for thought-forms: other people, future events, and the Transcendent Self.

💡 A well-formed thought-form must be emotionally charged, attached to a thread, and projected with confidence.

💡 The next section will cover how to strengthen thought-forms to ensure they continue influencing reality over time.

Section 7 – Strengthening Thought-Forms for Greater Influence

Now that you have trained the subconscious self to **send thought-forms through subconscious threads**, the next step is **ensuring that those thought-forms remain active and continue influencing reality.**

Many people unknowingly **weaken their own manifestations** by:
✗ Doubting their thought-forms after sending them.
✗ Attaching mixed emotions that distort the transmission.
✗ Failing to reinforce the thought-form with continued energy.

A thought-form is **not just an idea—it is an energetic construct** that must be:
✓ Maintained long enough for the subconscious self to fully transmit it.
✓ Reinforced with emotional energy so it remains active.
✓ Protected from external interference or self-sabotage.

By learning how to **strengthen and sustain thought-forms**, you ensure that **they continue influencing reality long after they are sent.**

Why Thought-Forms Fade or Lose Power

Even a **perfectly formed** thought-form can lose effectiveness if:

✗ **The subconscious self lacks enough energy to sustain it.**

✗ **The sender revisits it with doubt, which weakens its structure.**

✗ **External influences introduce conflicting energies that disrupt it.**

For a thought-form to manifest successfully, it must be:

✓ **Held steady in the subconscious self long enough for transmission.**

✓ **Reinforced with high-energy emotions.**

✓ **Released with full trust, avoiding interference.**

Mastering **thought-form reinforcement** ensures that manifestations are **not only sent but also received and acted upon.**

Three Techniques for Strengthening Thought-Forms

A well-formed thought-form is like a **seed planted in the soil of reality**—it needs **nourishment, protection, and time to grow.**

The following three techniques **reinforce thought-forms, making them more stable, resilient, and powerful.**

---

1 The Pulse Technique: Sending Energy Waves to Thought-Forms

Every thought-form needs **a sustained energy source** to remain active. The subconscious self can **strengthen existing thought-forms** by periodically sending **pulses of energy** to them.

How to Use the Pulse Technique

147

1 **Enter a relaxed alpha state** and recall the thought-form you previously sent.
2 **Visualize it in front of you as a glowing sphere, still connected to its target.**
3 **With each breath, send a pulse of energy toward it, reinforcing its structure.**
4 **Charge it with gratitude, certainty, and unwavering belief.**
5 **See it becoming brighter, stronger, and more vibrant.**

✅ **Best Use:** The Pulse Technique is ideal for **long-term manifestations** that require continued reinforcement, such as career success, relationship building, or healing intentions.

---

2 The Shielding Technique: Protecting Thought-Forms from Interference

Once a thought-form is sent, it may encounter **external influences** that weaken or disrupt it. This could come from:
✗ **Contradictory subconscious beliefs (e.g., fear of failure).**
✗ **Negative influences from other people's energy fields.**
✗ **Unconscious doubts that corrode the manifestation.**

To protect a thought-form, the subconscious self must **encase it in a shielded energetic structure**, preventing outside interference.

How to Use the Shielding Technique

1 **Recall the thought-form in the alpha state.**
2 **Visualize a protective field forming around it—this could be a golden sphere, a crystalline shield, or a cocoon of light.**
3 **Affirm with conviction:**

- *"This thought-form is completely shielded and remains intact until its full manifestation."*
  4 **Feel the energy field becoming solid and impenetrable.**
  5 **Release it, knowing it is protected from distortion.**

✅ **Best Use:** The Shielding Technique is effective for **high-value manifestations** that may be vulnerable to **self-doubt, negative external energy, or subconscious conflicts** (e.g., financial success, personal breakthroughs, or major life changes).

---

3 The Expansion Technique: Amplifying Thought-Forms to Influence Reality Faster

The Expansion Technique increases a thought-form's **size, reach, and intensity**, making it **stronger and more effective** in influencing reality.

How to Use the Expansion Technique

1 **Enter the alpha state and recall the thought-form.**
2 **Visualize it expanding in size, growing larger and more powerful.**
3 **Feel its presence radiating outward, touching everything in its path.**
4 **See it merging with reality, becoming an undeniable force.**
5 **Affirm with power:**

- *"This thought-form is now amplified and fully integrated into my reality."*
  6 **Release it, knowing it is now operating at full strength.**

✅ **Best Use:** The Expansion Technique is ideal for **manifestations that require rapid influence**, such as urgent opportunities, immediate solutions, or breakthroughs in personal and professional growth.

How to Know If a Thought-Form Is Fully Strengthened
A fully reinforced thought-form will exhibit **clear signs** that it has been successfully projected:
✓ **You feel a deep sense of certainty and peace about it.**
✓ **You notice synchronicities related to your manifestation.**

✓ Opportunities and events begin aligning effortlessly with your intention.

✓ You intuitively sense that "it is done," without needing to check on it.

If any of these signs are missing, **use one of the three reinforcement techniques** to ensure your thought-form remains strong and active.

The Next Step: Integrating Thought-Form Projection into Daily Life

Now that you understand how to **strengthen and protect thought-forms**, the final step is learning how to **integrate these skills into your everyday reality** so that:

✓ **Every thought you send is precise, powerful, and effective.**

✓ **You naturally align with a reality where manifestation happens fluidly.**

✓ **The subconscious self automatically reinforces thought-forms without effort.**

The next section will explore **how to create a daily subconscious training routine** that integrates:

✓ **Alpha-state manifestation practices.**

✓ **Thought-form reinforcement techniques.**

✓ **Subconscious alignment strategies to remove resistance.**

By developing a **systematic approach to thought-form projection**, you will enter a state where **manifestation becomes effortless, predictable, and second nature.**

Key Takeaways from This Section

💡 **A thought-form is an energetic construct that must be maintained, reinforced, and protected.**

💡 **Without reinforcement, thought-forms can fade or become distorted by external influences.**

💡 The three reinforcement techniques (Pulse, Shielding, Expansion) ensure that thought-forms remain active and effective.

💡 The next section will explore how to integrate thought-form projection into a daily subconscious training routine.

Section 8 – Integrating Thought-Form Projection into Daily Life

Now that you have mastered the process of **creating, projecting, and reinforcing thought-forms**, the final step is integrating these practices into your **daily subconscious training routine**.

A strong subconscious self does not rely on **sporadic bursts of intention**—it operates with **consistent, structured reinforcement** so that thought-form projection becomes as natural as breathing.

In this section, we will establish a **daily system** that ensures:
✓ **Your subconscious self automatically maintains, strengthens, and directs thought-forms.**
✓ **Manifestation becomes effortless and predictable.**
✓ **You remain in a state of alignment, where miracles unfold as a natural consequence of your trained subconscious processes.**

Why Consistency is the Key to Subconscious Mastery
Manifestation is not about **one-time effort**—it is about **sustained focus, energy, and alignment.**

✗ Many people fail at manifestation because they treat it as an **occasional practice**, rather than an **integrated subconscious habit.**
✗ If you only create and reinforce thought-forms **when you need something**, your subconscious self will remain untrained and inconsistent.
☑ When you practice **daily**, the subconscious self becomes a **constant transmitter of high-energy thought-forms**, making manifestation second nature.

By developing a **structured daily subconscious routine**, you ensure that:
✓ **Thought-forms remain active and well-supported.**
✓ **The subconscious self continuously refines its ability to send and receive transmissions.**
✓ **You maintain a state of alignment where manifestation happens fluidly.**

The Four-Part Daily Thought-Form Training Routine
To integrate subconscious training into daily life, use the **Four-Part Thought-Form Routine**, which takes just **15–20 minutes per day.**

Each part of this practice **reinforces subconscious mastery**, making it easier to:
✓ **Enter the alpha state on command.**
✓ **Project thought-forms automatically.**
✓ **Recognize and act on intuitive feedback.**

---

1 Morning Activation – Setting the Subconscious Focus for the Day

The moment **right after waking up** is when the subconscious self is **most impressionable**—before the conscious mind fully engages in daily distractions.

Morning Activation Steps:

1 **Before getting out of bed, take five deep breaths to relax the body.**
2 **Recall the main thought-form you are working on manifesting.**
3 **Engage the multi-sensory mental video (from Chapter 3) to experience the thought-form as already real.**
4 **Affirm with certainty:**

- *"This is my reality now. My subconscious self fully supports its unfolding."*

5 Feel gratitude as if the manifestation has already happened.

✅ **Why This Works:** This morning reinforcement ensures that the subconscious self begins the day **already aligned** with your intended manifestation.

---

2 Midday Alignment – Maintaining Thought-Form Strength

Throughout the day, distractions and external influences may **weaken your subconscious alignment** if not consciously maintained.

The Midday Alignment ensures that thought-forms remain **active and energized** while preventing interference from daily stresses.

Midday Alignment Steps (2–5 minutes):

1 **Pause and take three deep breaths to reset your awareness.**
2 **Silently recall your thought-form and visualize it as a glowing sphere of energy.**
3 **Mentally pulse energy to the thought-form (using the Pulse Technique from Section 7).**
4 **Affirm:**

- *"This thought-form is strong, vibrant, and fully manifesting."*
  5 **Return to your activities, knowing the thought-form remains active.**

✅ **Why This Works:** This quick midday practice prevents subconscious drift, keeping your thought-forms strong and undisturbed.

---

3 Evening Reinforcement – Deepening Subconscious Programming

The **pre-sleep state** is another powerful window where the subconscious self is highly receptive.

153

By reinforcing thought-forms before sleep, the subconscious self **works on them throughout the night**, strengthening their energetic imprint.

Evening Reinforcement Steps:

1 **Relax in bed and enter the alpha state using slow breathing.**
2 **Replay your multi-sensory mental video, feeling every detail as real.**
3 **Use the Expansion Technique (from Section 7) to amplify the thought-form's reach.**
4 **Surrender the thought-form to the Transcendent Self, trusting in its perfect unfolding.**
5 **Affirm:**

- *"As I sleep, my subconscious self and the Transcendent Self continue to manifest this reality."*

✅ **Why This Works:** Evening reinforcement ensures that the subconscious self **remains engaged with the thought-form overnight**, allowing for deeper integration.

---

4 Intuitive Tracking – Recognizing and Responding to Synchronicities

The final part of daily subconscious training is learning to **actively recognize and interpret feedback from the Transcendent Self.**

Synchronicities, gut feelings, or sudden insights are often **direct confirmations** that thought-forms are influencing reality.

Intuitive Tracking Steps:
1 **At the end of each day, review any synchronicities or intuitive impressions you noticed.**
2 **Write down patterns, recurring symbols, or unexpected events that align with your manifestation.**
3 **Acknowledge and express gratitude for each sign, reinforcing your subconscious confidence.**

☑ **Why This Works:** Tracking synchronicities **increases subconscious sensitivity to manifestation feedback**, making it easier to act on guidance.

The Final Shift: Living as a Subconscious Master
By integrating this **daily subconscious training**, you shift from:
✗ **Occasional manifestation efforts** → **to a continuous subconscious process.**
✗ **Wishing for change** → **to creating reality through structured subconscious training.**
✗ **Hoping for miracles** → **to generating them as a natural function of subconscious mastery.**

Over time, the subconscious self becomes so well-trained that:
✓ **Thought-forms are projected and reinforced automatically.**
✓ **Manifestation feels effortless because subconscious resistance is eliminated.**
✓ **Reality begins responding in real-time to the subconscious self's refined transmissions.**

When the subconscious self operates at this level, **miracles don't just happen occasionally—they happen predictably.**

The Next Step: Synchronizing the Conscious, Subconscious, and Transcendent Self
Now that you have fully developed the subconscious self's ability to **send, receive, and sustain thought-forms,** the final step in subconscious training is **harmonizing all three parts of the human system—the conscious self, subconscious self, and Transcendent Self.**

This integration is what allows for:
✓ **Complete alignment between thought, energy, and external reality.**

✓ Instantaneous manifestation with minimal effort.
✓ A state of flow where reality continuously adjusts to support your desires.

The next chapter will further explore **non-local communication between persons** ensuring that all three aspects of the self function as a **unified force** in shaping reality.

Because when all three are in perfect harmony, **manifestation becomes effortless, and you step into full mastery of the Science of Miracles.**

Key Takeaways from This Section

💡 A structured daily subconscious training routine ensures that manifestation becomes second nature.

💡 The Four-Part Routine (Morning Activation, Midday Alignment, Evening Reinforcement, and Intuitive Tracking) optimizes subconscious programming.

💡 By integrating thought-form projection into daily life, the subconscious self naturally operates at a high level.

💡 The next step is synchronizing the conscious self, subconscious self, and Transcendent Self for full manifestation power.

Section 9 – The Transition to Full Subconscious Mastery

At this stage, you have developed a **powerful, well-trained subconscious self** that:

✓ **Generates and sustains thought-forms with clarity and emotional charge.**

✓ **Projects thought-forms outward through subconscious threads to influence reality.**

✓ **Reinforces and protects manifestations to ensure they remain active.**

✓ **Operates within a structured daily routine to maintain alignment.**

This marks a **fundamental shift**—no longer are you **reacting to reality**; instead, your subconscious self is actively **shaping reality in accordance with your desires.**

In this final section of subconscious training, we will examine:
✓ **How to recognize when subconscious mastery has been fully achieved.**
✓ **The natural signs that your subconscious self is functioning at its highest level.**
✓ **How to maintain long-term subconscious alignment with the Transcendent Self.**

This is where you step into **a life where miracles are no longer rare events but natural, predictable, and continuous.**

Signs of Full Subconscious Mastery
How do you know when your subconscious self has reached the level of **consistent, effortless manifestation?**

Here are the key signs that your subconscious self is operating at **full power:**

✓ **Manifestations Occur Quickly and Predictably**

- Thought-forms materialize with **less effort and more speed** than ever before.

- You no longer feel the need to "force" results; instead, you expect them with certainty.

✓ **You Receive Immediate Synchronicities as Confirmation**

- The moment you **project a thought-form**, you begin noticing signs aligning with your request.

- Reality starts responding **in real time**—people, opportunities, and resources appear effortlessly.

✓ Subconscious Alignment Becomes Automatic

- You no longer need to **"remind" yourself to stay in alignment**—it happens naturally.
- Your subconscious self instantly **filters out negative influences and conflicting thought-forms.**

✓ Your Emotional State Remains Stable and High-Vibration

- Since **emotion is the fuel of manifestation**, a well-trained subconscious self keeps you **centered in joy, gratitude, and certainty.**
- Even when challenges arise, you remain **calm and focused**, knowing that you can shift reality from within.

✓ Intuitive Guidance is Strong, Clear, and Immediate

- Your subconscious self **transmits insights from the Transcendent Self without interference.**
- You have an inner knowing of **what actions to take, whom to connect with, and which opportunities to pursue.**

When all these signs are present, you have entered the realm of **subconscious mastery**, where **thought, energy, and reality move in perfect harmony.**

Long-Term Maintenance of Subconscious Mastery
Even after achieving full subconscious alignment, **ongoing maintenance is necessary** to ensure that your abilities remain strong.

Here's how to maintain subconscious mastery for life:

✓ Refine and Expand Your Thought-Form Skills

- As your subconscious self strengthens, experiment with **more complex manifestations, faster timelines, and greater precision.**

✓ **Stay in a High-Energy Emotional State**

- Since emotion fuels manifestation, continue practicing **gratitude, joy, and certainty** daily.

- If negative emotions arise, use **the Personal Demon Demolisher (from Chapter 7) to clear subconscious interference.**

✓ **Continue Strengthening Subconscious Threads**

- Maintain strong etheric connections to **desired outcomes, people, and locations** to ensure manifestation flow remains uninterrupted.

✓ **Trust the Transcendent Self Completely**

- Let go of **attachment to outcomes**—when you trust the process fully, manifestations unfold **with perfect timing and precision.**

When subconscious mastery becomes a **way of being**, you move beyond **training** into **living as a deliberate creator of reality.**

Final Integration: The Role of the Subconscious Self in the Three-Self System

The subconscious self does not operate in isolation—it functions as part of a **three-self system**, working in harmony with:

✓ **The Conscious Self** – The initiator of desires, decisions, and logical action.

✓ **The Subconscious Self** – The bridge between thought and reality, transmitting thought-forms.

✓ **The Transcendent Self** – The ultimate receiver and executor of manifestations.

To achieve **total mastery of the Science of Miracles**, the next step is ensuring that **all three selves work in unified alignment.**

The next chapter will explore the **final integration process**, where:
✔ **The conscious self sets the vision with complete clarity.**
✔ **The subconscious self transmits thought-forms effortlessly.**
✔ **The Transcendent Self responds instantly, shaping reality in your favor.**

When these three aspects function as **one**, you move beyond subconscious mastery into **total life mastery**, where:
✔ **Manifestation is no longer something you "practice"—it is simply the way you exist.**
✔ **Miracles happen daily, effortlessly, and with absolute certainty.**
✔ **You embody the full power of Mastering the Science of Miracles®.**

Key Takeaways from This Section
💡 **Subconscious mastery is achieved when manifestation becomes predictable, fast, and effortless.**
💡 **Signs of subconscious mastery include synchronicities, emotional stability, and automatic alignment.**
💡 **Ongoing subconscious training ensures long-term manifestation power.**
💡 **The final step is integrating the conscious self, subconscious self, and Transcendent Self into a unified force.**

Section 10 – The Final Transition: Preparing for Full Three-Self Integration

Now that you have achieved **subconscious mastery**, you stand at the threshold of the final transformation—**integrating the subconscious self into a fully unified system** with the conscious self and the Transcendent Self.

This marks the shift from **individual subconscious training** to **whole-being synchronization**, where:
✓ **The conscious self** directs with clarity and certainty.
✓ **The subconscious self** transmits thought-forms with power and precision.
✓ **The Transcendent Self** receives, amplifies, and manifests those thought-forms into reality.

When these three aspects work together seamlessly, **manifestation is no longer something you "do"—it becomes the natural function of your being.**

Why Three-Self Integration is Essential for Ultimate Manifestation Power
Even though you have now **trained the subconscious self to project thought-forms effectively**, subconscious mastery alone is **not enough**—the full power of manifestation only emerges when:
✓ **The conscious self is in alignment** (clear in its desires and free from contradictory intentions).
✓ **The subconscious self is open and cooperative** (acting as a willing bridge between thought and reality).
✓ **The Transcendent Self is fully engaged** (receiving and responding without interference).

If any of these elements are **out of sync**, manifestation becomes:
✗ **Slow and inconsistent** (if the subconscious self resists or is not fully trained).
✗ **Blocked or misdirected** (if the conscious self sends mixed signals).
✗ **Disconnected from higher forces** (if the Transcendent Self is not engaged in the process).

When all three selves are in harmony, manifestation shifts from **occasional success** to a **constant flow of miracles.**

The Process of Subconscious Integration with the Three-Self System

To integrate the subconscious self fully into the three-self system, we will follow a **step-by-step synchronization process** that ensures:

✓ **The conscious self communicates clearly.**

✓ **The subconscious self is fully aligned and free of resistance.**

✓ **The Transcendent Self becomes a continuous source of guidance and power.**

The following integration techniques will finalize **subconscious alignment** and prepare for **full three-self mastery** in the next chapter.

---

1 Unifying the Subconscious and Conscious Self for Absolute Clarity

The subconscious self thrives on **clear, single-focus commands**—yet many people send **mixed messages** that confuse or weaken manifestation.

For example:

✗ You set the intention for financial abundance but subconsciously believe money is difficult to attain.

✗ You project a thought-form of success but carry emotional patterns of fear and failure.

The subconscious self is **obedient**—if it receives **conflicting messages**, it cancels them out, making manifestation **slow or ineffective.**

Alignment Technique: The Single-Line Command Process

To align the subconscious and conscious self, use the **Single-Line Command Process**:

1 **Write down your core manifestation goal in a single, clear statement.**

- Example: *"I am a powerful manifester, attracting wealth, joy, and abundance effortlessly."*

2 Scan for subconscious resistance—does any doubt, fear, or hesitation arise?

- If yes, it must be cleared before the subconscious self can fully engage.

3 Reframe the subconscious belief to support the goal.

- Example: If resistance arises (*"What if I fail?"*), reframe it as *"My subconscious self is fully trained, and my success is inevitable."*

4 Repeat the single-line command daily in an alpha state until the subconscious fully accepts it.

✅ **Why This Works:** This process eliminates subconscious contradictions, ensuring that **all manifestations are received as absolute truth.**

---

2 Strengthening the Connection Between the Subconscious and Transcendent Self

Even with a well-trained subconscious self, **manifestation is amplified exponentially when the Transcendent Self is fully engaged.**

The **Transcendent Self operates beyond time and space**, responding instantly to:
✓ **Well-formed thought-forms.**
✓ **High-energy emotional frequencies.**
✓ **Unwavering certainty from the subconscious self.**

To ensure the **subconscious self maintains an open and direct channel** with the Transcendent Self, practice the following **Alignment Meditation**:

Alignment Meditation: The Light Channel Connection

1 **Enter a deep alpha state through relaxed breathing.**
2 **Visualize a golden light descending from above, representing the Transcendent Self.**
3 **See this light merging into your subconscious self, creating an unbreakable connection.**
4 **Affirm:**

- *"My subconscious self and the Transcendent Self are one. My desires are heard and fulfilled instantly."*
  5 **Feel the energy of certainty and divine alignment filling your entire being.**

✅ **Why This Works:** This meditation strengthens the **two-way connection** between the subconscious and Transcendent Self, ensuring that all manifestations are received without interference.

---

3 Moving from Effortful Manifestation to Automatic Manifestation

As the subconscious self becomes fully integrated into the three-self system, manifestation becomes:
✓ **Instantaneous** – Thought-forms materialize faster because there is no internal resistance.
✓ **Effortless** – You no longer have to "try" to manifest—your subconscious self does it automatically.
✓ **Predictable** – Reality becomes a mirror of your inner alignment, responding exactly as expected.

At this level of mastery:
✓ **You don't just visualize success—you expect it.**
✓ **You don't hope for miracles—you generate them.**
✓ **You don't wish for change—you direct it at will.**

This is the state of **full subconscious integration**, where **the boundary between thought and reality dissolves, and miracles become your natural state of existence.**

Final Preparation for Three-Self Synchronization

With the subconscious self now fully trained and aligned, the next chapter will **finalize the full integration of the Three Selves**, ensuring that:

✓ **The conscious self operates from complete clarity and confidence.**

✓ **The subconscious self functions as an effortless bridge between thought and reality.**

✓ **The Transcendent Self responds instantly, shaping reality in real time.**

This is where you step into **the highest level of manifestation mastery**—where you no longer seek miracles because **you are the source of them.**

Key Takeaways from This Section

💡 **Subconscious mastery is fully realized when it aligns seamlessly with both the conscious and Transcendent Self.**

💡 **The Single-Line Command Process ensures that the subconscious self only receives clear, unwavering instructions.**

💡 **Strengthening the subconscious-Transcendent Self connection amplifies manifestation power.**

💡 **Full subconscious integration leads to instant, effortless, and predictable manifestations.**

💡 **The next chapter will focus on non-local contact between persons.**

Chapter 6: Non-Local Contact Between Persons

Section 1 – Expanding Subconscious Communication

In previous chapters, you developed the ability to project your subconscious self beyond the physical senses, using techniques such as sensory projection and thought-form transmission (*see Chapters 4 and 5*). Now, you will take the next step: sending and receiving non-local messages between individuals.

Non-local communication is not a mystical phenomenon—it is a natural function of the subconscious self. In *Chapter 5*, we explored how the subconscious self maintains aka thread connections between people, objects, and places. These etheric connections are the same pathways through which non-local messages travel.

Most people already experience passive non-local moments without realizing it:
✓ Thinking about someone just before they call or text.
✓ Sensing a loved one's emotions from afar.
✓ Feeling a sudden "knowing" about a situation without logical reasoning.

These are examples of the subconscious self receiving non-local impressions without deliberate effort. In this chapter, you will learn how to:
✓ Move from passive reception to active, intentional non-local communication.
✓ Train the subconscious self to send and receive messages with clarity.
✓ Strengthen the aka thread connection for instant, accurate transmissions.

Just as you trained your subconscious self to project thought-forms for manifestation (*see Chapter 3*), you will now train it to transmit and receive information non-locally. The process follows the same fundamental principles:

✓ A thought-form must be well-structured and emotionally charged.
✓ Aka threads serve as the transmission lines for sending and receiving messages.
✓ A strong energy charge is required for clear transmission.

If you have not yet practiced the energy-building exercises from Chapter 3, revisit them now, as they are essential for strengthening your non-local abilities.

With this foundation in place, the first step is learning how to communicate with the subconscious self in its own language—a necessary skill for both sending and receiving non-local messages.

Key Takeaways from This Section

💡 Non-local communication is a natural extension of subconscious projection and aka thread connections.

💡 Most people experience passive non-local moments, but training allows for deliberate, repeatable communication.

💡 Non-local messages follow the same principles as thought-form projection—clear structure, strong emotional charge, and an activated transmission line.

💡 The next step is learning to communicate with the subconscious self in its own language to ensure accurate non-local reception.

Section 2 – Learning to Communicate with the Subconscious Self in Its Own Language

As covered in *Chapter 4*, the subconscious self does not process information in words and abstract logic as the conscious self does. Instead, it communicates through:

✓ **Images and symbols** – Vivid mental pictures, archetypal symbols, and dream-like visuals.
✓ **Emotions and sensations** – Feelings that arise in response to incoming impressions.

✓ **Intuitive knowing** – Immediate awareness of information without conscious reasoning.

For non-local communication to be **accurate and reliable**, you must train your subconscious self to **send and receive messages in its natural format** rather than attempting to impose conscious thought structures onto it.

How the Subconscious Self Processes Information

In *Chapter 4*, we used the **analogy of training a highly intelligent service animal** to describe the subconscious self. It follows **clear, direct commands** but does not understand **long explanations or abstract reasoning**.

The same principle applies to non-local communication. If you attempt to send or receive messages in **long sentences or logical sequences**, the subconscious self will struggle to process them. However, if you work with:
✓ **Simple symbols and sensory impressions**,
✓ **Emotionally charged thought-forms**, and
✓ **Clear energetic intent**,

...then non-local communication becomes effortless and precise.

Training the Subconscious Self to Receive Non-local Messages

Since the subconscious self is **already receiving** non-local impressions constantly, training is less about **starting** the process and more about **refining awareness and focus**.

To develop this skill, revisit *Exercise 1: Strengthening Subconscious Reception with Symbol Recognition* from *Chapter 4*, which helps condition the subconscious self to **register and interpret incoming symbolic messages**.

For non-local training, apply the same technique but modify it for receiving information from another person:

Non-local Adaptation of the Symbol Recognition Exercise
1 **Enter a relaxed alpha state** (*see Chapter 4 for induction techniques*).
2 **Set the intention:**

- *"I am now open to receiving non-local symbols from [partner's name]."*
  3 **Observe the first impression that appears—do not filter or analyze it.**
  4 **Write or sketch the symbol, then compare with your partner's transmitted message.**

By **repeating and refining** this process, the subconscious self learns to **focus non-local reception** on a specific source rather than picking up random impressions.

Preventing Interference from the Logical Mind

As covered in *Chapter 4*, one of the biggest challenges in working with the subconscious self is **interference from the logical mind**.

In non-local communication, this manifests as:
X **Doubting the first impression and assuming it was "just imagination."**
X **Overanalyzing received messages instead of allowing them to flow naturally.**
X **Forcing responses instead of trusting the subconscious self to deliver them.**

To prevent interference:
✓ **Write down impressions immediately** before your conscious mind starts analyzing them.
✓ **Trust the first impression**—it is usually the correct non-local reception.
✓ **Avoid forcing an answer**—relax and allow messages to surface naturally.

The Next Step: Building an Energy Reserve for Non-local Transmission

Now that you understand how to **receive non-local messages**, the next step is ensuring that you have enough **vital life energy** to send messages with clarity and strength.

In *Chapter 3*, we covered how **vital life energy serves as the carrier wave** for thought-forms and subconscious transmissions. The next section will focus on **how to build and maintain a high-energy charge** to ensure that your non-local messages are strong, clear, and reliably received.

Key Takeaways from This Section

💡 The subconscious self communicates in symbols, emotions, and intuitive impressions, not words or logic.

💡 Training the subconscious self for non-local reception requires focusing on first impressions and avoiding over-analysis.

💡 Symbol recognition exercises (see Chapter 4) are essential for refining non-local accuracy.

💡 The next step is learning to generate and store enough energy for effective non-local transmission.

Section 3 – Building a Surplus Charge of Vital Life Energy

Now that you understand how to **receive non-local messages**, the next step is ensuring that you have enough **vital life energy** to send messages with clarity and strength.

Non-local transmission is not just about **mental focus**—it requires a **strong charge of energy** to carry the thought-form from your subconscious self to another person. Without this energy, messages may be **weak, distorted, or fail to reach the intended recipient.**

As covered in *Chapter 3: The Energy of Miracles*, **vital life energy (qi, prana, aka energy)** serves as the **carrier wave** for thought-forms, whether for manifestation or non-local transmission. The subconscious self **administers and directs this energy**, making it essential to train and refine this ability.

If you have not yet mastered the **energy-building practices** from *Chapter 3*, revisit them now. Without sufficient energy reserves, non-local communication will be unreliable.

This section will focus specifically on **how to apply energy-building techniques to non-local work**, ensuring that every transmission is **strong, direct, and accurately received.**

Why Non-local Transmission Requires Energy

As discussed in *Chapter 3*, the subconscious self regulates **vital life energy** across all levels—**physical, mental, emotional, and spiritual.** In the context of non-local communication, this energy is essential because:

✓ **It strengthens the aka thread connection** between sender and receiver.
✓ **It powers the thought-form transmission**, ensuring clarity and focus.
✓ **It prevents mental fatigue**, allowing for longer, more sustained communication.

Just as a **radio requires sufficient power to broadcast a clear signal**, non-local messages require an **energetic charge** to ensure they reach their target without distortion.

Adapting Energy Cultivation to Non-local Work

In *Chapter 3*, you learned foundational exercises such as **Lower Dan Tian Charging** and **The Energy Circulation Loop**. These practices are the basis for increasing the subconscious self's ability to **store and direct energy efficiently.**

Before practicing **non-local transmission**, integrate the following adaptations to maximize effectiveness:

1 Lower Dan Tian Charging for Non-Local Communication

(See Chapter 3 for full instructions on Lower Dan Tian Charging.)

Application for Non-local Work:
✓ Perform **5–10 minutes of Lower Dan Tian breathing** before sending or receiving messages.
✓ As you breathe in, visualize energy **building in the Lower Dan Tian and flowing toward your head and hands**, strengthening your non-local output.
✓ When preparing to send a message, feel the energy **gathering behind your forehead** (third eye area), intensifying the transmission.

☑ **Why This Works:** Strengthening the Lower Dan Tian ensures that the subconscious self has a **stable energy reservoir** to power non-local projection.

---

2 Energy Circulation to Prevent Blockages

(See Chapter 3 for full instructions on The Energy Circulation Loop.)

Application for Non-local Work:
✓ Before sending a message, circulate energy **through your spine and hands**, ensuring the energy pathways are clear.
✓ Before receiving a message, circulate energy **through your heart center and forehead**, making you more sensitive to incoming transmissions.
✓ If energy feels stagnant or weak, return to basic circulation practices before continuing.

☑ **Why This Works:** Ensuring **smooth energy flow** prevents blockages that can interfere with non-local clarity and reception.

Additional Practices for Strengthening Non-local Transmission
Once a solid **energy foundation** is in place, the following exercises
will further enhance your ability to **send and receive non-local
messages effectively.**

Exercise: Charging the Aka Thread for Stronger Non-local Contact

As explained in *Chapter 5: Developing the Secret Skills of the
Subconscious Self*, the subconscious self uses **aka threads** to maintain
energetic connections between individuals. These threads act as **the
transmission lines** for non-local messages.

Steps to Charge the Aka Thread for Non-local Sending:

1 **Enter the Alpha State** (*See Chapter 4 for alpha induction
techniques*).
2 **Visualize an aka thread connecting you to the intended
recipient.**
3 **Breathe deeply and send energy along the aka thread,
reinforcing the connection.**
4 **Feel the thread strengthening, ensuring a clear, undistorted
link.**

✅ **Why This Works:**
✓ Strengthening the aka thread **reduces interference**, allowing
messages to travel directly to the recipient.
✓ It ensures that the message does not dissipate before reaching its
destination.

(*For more on aka threads, refer to Chapter 5.*)

How to Know If You Have Enough Energy for Non-local Work If you
experience **any of the following signs**, your subconscious self is

signaling that your energy reserves are **too low** for non-local transmission:

✗ Mental fatigue or difficulty holding a clear thought-form.
✗ Weak, fragmented messages that feel "distant" or unclear.
✗ Difficulty maintaining focus or feeling easily distracted.

In this case, **pause non-local practice** and return to the **energy-building exercises from Chapter 3** until your reserves are replenished.

When your **energy is fully charged**, non-local transmission will feel:
✓ Effortless and clear, with no mental strain.
✓ Strong and vivid, as if the message is being "pushed" rather than "pulled."
✓ Direct and focused, without interference from stray thoughts.

The Next Step: Understanding the Aka Thread Connection in Non-local Transmission
Now that you have learned how to **build and store energy**, the next section will focus on:

✓ **How aka threads function as the subconscious "transmission lines" for non-local messages.**
✓ **The science behind instant subconscious communication across distance.**
✓ **How to consciously activate aka threads to strengthen non-local accuracy.**

Mastering **aka thread transmission** ensures that your non-local messages **travel with clarity and reach the intended recipient without interference.**

Key Takeaways from This Section
💡 **Non-local transmission requires a surplus charge of energy— without it, messages are weak or unclear.**

💡 The subconscious self regulates and directs energy—strengthening its reserves is essential for effective non-local communication.

💡 Energy-building exercises from Chapter 3 provide the foundation for non-local strength—return to them as needed.

💡 Charging the aka thread strengthens the connection between sender and receiver, ensuring clear transmission.

💡 The next step is learning how aka threads function as non-local transmission lines.

Section 4 – Transmission Lines as Symbols of Aka Threads

In *Chapter 5*, we explored how the subconscious self maintains **aka thread connections**—etheric pathways that link people, places, and thought-forms across time and space. These same aka threads serve as the **transmission lines for non-local messages**.

Understanding aka threads is essential for mastering non-local contact because:

✔ They are **the energetic highways** that carry thought-forms between sender and receiver.

✔ They function **outside of space and time**, allowing instant communication regardless of distance.

✔ The **stronger the thread, the clearer and more reliable the transmission**.

If you have not yet practiced **activating and strengthening aka threads**, review *Chapter 5* before continuing. Without a stable thread connection, non-local messages may be **weak, unclear, or fail to reach the intended target**.

Aka Threads and the Science of Instant Communication

Although aka threads operate at the **subconscious and energetic**

level, their function is strikingly similar to modern **wireless communication networks**:

✓ **Like fiber-optic cables carry digital signals**, aka threads carry thought-forms between minds.
✓ **Like Wi-Fi signals travel invisibly between devices**, aka transmissions occur without the need for physical proximity.
✓ **Like quantum entanglement suggests instant information transfer**, aka threads allow for immediate non-local contact, regardless of distance.

Because these threads are **woven through repeated interaction**, you already have **pre-existing aka connections** with:
✓ People you are emotionally close to (family, friends, mentors).
✓ Those with whom you have had frequent past interactions.
✓ Individuals with whom you have **strong emotional experiences**, whether positive or negative.

This is why spontaneous non-local moments often occur **between close friends, romantic partners, or family members**—their aka threads are naturally stronger due to **consistent energetic exchange over time**.

The goal of non-local training is to:
✓ **Strengthen and reinforce existing aka threads for clearer transmission.**
✓ **Create new aka threads for deliberate communication with specific individuals.**
✓ **Consciously activate aka threads before sending or receiving a non-local message.**

Strengthening the Aka Thread Connection for Non-local Work
To ensure a **clear and uninterrupted transmission**, the aka thread must be **activated and charged** before sending a non-local message. This process is similar to **tuning a radio frequency**—it sharpens the connection, making it easier for both sender and receiver to exchange thought-forms.

Exercise: Activating the Aka Thread for Non-local Sending

1 **Enter a relaxed alpha state** (*see Chapter 4 for induction techniques*).
2 **Visualize an aka thread connecting you to the recipient, glowing with energy.**
3 **Breathe deeply, sending energy along the thread to reinforce the connection.**
4 **Hold the image for a few moments, sensing the energetic link becoming stronger.**
5 **Once the thread feels stable, proceed with sending the non-local message.**

✅ **Why This Works:**
✓ Reinforcing the aka thread **prepares the subconscious self** for direct communication.
✓ It **filters out background noise**, ensuring the message reaches only the intended recipient.
✓ A well-charged aka thread allows **faster, clearer, and more precise non-local exchanges.**

How to Know If an Aka Thread Is Weak or Disrupted
A weak or disrupted aka thread can cause:
✗ **Fuzzy, unclear transmissions** where the message lacks detail.
✗ **Interference from unrelated impressions**, making it hard to distinguish the correct information.
✗ **Delayed or blocked messages**, where the thought-form does not seem to reach the recipient.

To repair and strengthen a weak aka thread:
✓ **Reinforce the connection daily** using the activation exercise.
✓ **Engage in direct communication with the person (verbal or energetic)** to refresh the thread.
✓ **Clear emotional blockages** that may be distorting the energetic link (*see Chapter 7: The Personal Demon Demolisher*).

Once the aka thread is strong, the next step is learning how to **prepare for sending and receiving non-local messages with precision.**

The Next Step: Preparation for Sending and Receiving Information

Now that you understand how **aka threads function as transmission lines**, the next section will focus on:

✓ The **best conditions for successful non-local contact** (mental state, location, timing).

✓ How to **optimize subconscious receptivity** before attempting non-local communication.

✓ Techniques to **eliminate interference and increase signal clarity.**

Without proper preparation, even a well-formed non-local message may be **weakened by external distractions or subconscious resistance.** The next section ensures that **every non-local exchange is structured for success.**

Key Takeaways from This Section

💡 **Aka threads act as the transmission lines for non-local messages, carrying thought-forms between minds.**

💡 **These threads already exist between people with emotional or energetic connections, but they must be consciously activated for clear communication.**

💡 **Strengthening an aka thread before non-local transmission ensures that messages are direct, accurate, and received without interference.**

💡 **A weak aka thread can result in unclear or distorted messages—daily reinforcement keeps it strong.**

💡 **The next step is preparing the subconscious self for sending and receiving non-local messages with maximum accuracy.**

Section 5 – Preparation for Sending and Receiving Information

Now that you understand how aka threads function as **transmission lines for non-local contact** (*see Chapter 5*), the next step is **optimizing conditions for successful communication.**

Non-local accuracy depends on several key factors:
✓ **Mental and emotional state** – A calm, focused mind enhances signal clarity.
✓ **Environmental factors** – Reducing distractions improves subconscious reception.
✓ **Subconscious alignment** – Ensuring that the subconscious self is receptive and engaged.

If you attempt non-local contact while **mentally scattered or emotionally unstable**, the subconscious self may struggle to maintain a **clear connection**, leading to distorted or weak transmissions. Proper preparation ensures that **messages are strong, direct, and accurately received.**

Choosing a Practice Partner

To develop precision in non-local sending and receiving, it is recommended to **practice with a trusted partner** before attempting long-distance communication.

✓ **Best practice partners** are individuals with whom you already have a **strong aka thread connection** (close friends, family members, or mentors).
✓ **Avoid skeptics or highly analytical individuals at first**—their logical resistance can interfere with non-local accuracy.
✓ **Once accuracy is established, you can expand practice to distant or unfamiliar individuals.**

Optimizing Your Mental State for Non-local Work

Just as an unstable radio signal can cause static interference, **mental** clutter and emotional turbulence can distort non-local communication.

Before attempting non-local contact:

1 **Enter an alpha state** (*see Chapter 4 for relaxation and induction techniques*).
2 **Clear mental distractions** by using a simple breathwork exercise (e.g., slow diaphragmatic breathing).
3 **Stabilize emotional energy** by focusing on **gratitude or inner stillness**—emotions act as amplifiers for non-local signals.
4 **Affirm your intention:**

- *"I am fully focused and open to clear, accurate non-local communication."*
  5 **If sending a message, visualize the recipient's aka thread becoming brighter and more active.**
  6 **If receiving a message, hold an open, receptive awareness—do not force an impression.**

✅ **Why This Works:**
✓ The subconscious self functions best in a **relaxed, focused state**, free from conscious interference.
✓ Emotional neutrality prevents **unwanted distortions or projections** from affecting the message.
✓ Strengthening intention **sharpens the aka thread**, ensuring a clear pathway for transmission.

Creating an Ideal Environment for Non-local Training
While non-local messages can be sent and received anywhere, **reducing environmental distractions** increases accuracy, especially in early practice sessions.

✓ **Choose a quiet, undisturbed space** where you will not be interrupted.
✓ **Dim lighting or close your eyes** to enhance internal focus.
✓ **Minimize electronic distractions**—excess electromagnetic noise

may disrupt sensitivity.
✓ **Sit or lie in a relaxed posture**, ensuring physical comfort.

Over time, the subconscious self will adapt to sending and receiving **even in chaotic environments**, but structured practice in **a controlled setting** will accelerate mastery.

The Best Types of Information to Send and Receive
To build confidence in non-local accuracy, start with **simple, concrete impressions** before progressing to complex ideas or emotions.

✓ **Basic geometric shapes** (e.g., circle, square, triangle).
✓ **Simple colors or single words.**
✓ **Visual images** (e.g., a tree, a house, an apple).
✓ **Emotional states** (e.g., happiness, calm, excitement).

Once accuracy is established, progress to:
✓ **Short phrases or sentences.**
✓ **More abstract concepts, such as intentions or moods.**
✓ **Personalized messages tailored to the receiver's thoughts.**

✅ **Why This Works:**
✓ The subconscious self responds best to **clear, recognizable forms** in early training.
✓ Starting with **simple messages reduces interference and strengthens confidence.**
✓ As subconscious receptivity improves, more detailed messages will be transmitted effortlessly.

The Next Step: The Receiving Process – How to Accurately Receive Non-local Messages
Now that you understand how to **prepare for non-local transmission**, the next section will cover:
✓ **How to ensure the subconscious self is fully receptive before attempting to receive a message.**

✓ Methods for verifying the accuracy of received impressions.

✓ How to distinguish between actual non-local messages and internal noise.

A well-prepared subconscious self is the **foundation for successful non-local reception**, ensuring that **messages arrive with clarity, accuracy, and minimal distortion.**

Key Takeaways from This Section

💡 Mental clarity, emotional stability, and environmental control enhance non-local accuracy.

💡 Choosing a trusted practice partner ensures a strong, pre-existing aka thread connection.

💡 Early practice should focus on simple, concrete impressions before advancing to complex messages.

💡 The next step is mastering the receiving process to ensure messages are interpreted correctly.

Section 6 – The Receiving Process: How to Accurately Receive Non-local Messages

Now that you have prepared your **mental state, environment, and aka thread connection** (*see Section 5*), the next step is learning how to **accurately receive non-local messages** without distortion.

Non-local reception is not about "guessing"—it is about **allowing the subconscious self to retrieve and present the message in its own way.** The key to accuracy is **trusting the first impression** and distinguishing between **true non-local reception and internal mental noise.**

How the Subconscious Self Receives Messages

As covered in *Chapter 4*, the subconscious self **does not communicate**

182

in words or logical sequences like the conscious self. Instead, it presents information as:

✓ **Images or symbols** – The received message may appear as a mental picture, an archetypal symbol, or a dream-like vision.
✓ **Emotions or sensations** – The energy of the sender's message may manifest as a **feeling** rather than a specific thought.
✓ **Intuitive knowing** – A sudden awareness of the message without conscious reasoning.

Messages may come in a **combination of these formats**, depending on how your subconscious self naturally processes information.

☑ **Example:** If your partner sends the word "tree," you might receive:
✓ A mental image of a tree.
✓ A sensation of standing under shade with a cool breeze.
✓ The word "tree" appearing suddenly in your mind.

Each response is valid—it simply depends on how your subconscious self **chooses to translate the message**.

Step-by-Step Process for Receiving a Non-local Message
To ensure **clarity and accuracy**, follow this structured approach when receiving a non-local message:

1 Enter a Relaxed, Receptive State

- Use **alpha induction techniques** (*see Chapter 4*) to calm the conscious mind and make space for subconscious impressions.

- Take **three slow, deep breaths**, focusing your awareness inward.

2 Activate the Aka Thread Connection

- Mentally acknowledge your link to the sender by visualizing the aka thread between you.

- Affirm: *"I am fully open to receiving this message clearly and accurately."*

3 Passively Observe the First Impression

- Do **not force an answer**—simply **observe** what arises.

- The first impression is usually the correct one. It may appear as:
  ✓ A **flash of imagery** (e.g., a bird, a color, a shape).
  ✓ A **subtle feeling or energy shift** (e.g., excitement, peace).
  ✓ A **word or phrase suddenly emerging in thought.**

4 Record the Impression Immediately

- **Write or sketch** what you receive **before your logical mind has time to analyze or doubt it**.

- If the message feels incomplete, note any additional **emotions, colors, or secondary impressions** that arise.

5 Confirm Accuracy with the Sender

- Compare your received impression with what was actually sent.

- Even if details are slightly different, focus on **patterns**—are you consistently picking up related themes or symbols?

✅ **Why This Works:**
✓ **Prevents logical interference**—by writing immediately, you bypass overthinking.
✓ **Strengthens subconscious confidence**—positive feedback reinforces non-local accuracy.
✓ **Trains subconscious focus**—repetition improves clarity over time.

Common Mistakes and How to Overcome Them
✗ **Overanalyzing the First Impression**

- **Mistake:** Assuming the first image or feeling is random or meaningless.

- **Solution:** Accept **whatever appears first**—analysis comes after validation with the sender.

✗ Forcing a Message Instead of Allowing It

- **Mistake:** Straining to "hear" something or trying to make sense of silence.

- **Solution:** Stay relaxed and **trust passive reception**—forcing blocks subconscious flow.

✗ Interference from the Logical Mind

- **Mistake:** Judging the message as "wrong" before confirming with the sender.

- **Solution:** Treat non-local reception like dream interpretation—symbols may be metaphorical rather than literal.

Strengthening Non-local Reception Over Time
If initial accuracy is inconsistent, practice the following:

✓ **Daily Symbol Recognition Training** (*see Chapter 4*) – Condition your subconscious self to recognize non-local symbols quickly.
✓ **Energy Sensitivity Exercises** (*see Chapter 3*) – Strengthen your ability to perceive subtle impressions.
✓ **Short, Focused Sessions** – Avoid mental fatigue by keeping non-local practice brief (5–10 minutes at first).

With consistent training, subconscious reception becomes **sharper, clearer, and faster**, making non-local contact a **predictable skill rather than a random event**.

The Next Step: The Sending Process – How to Transmit a Clear Thought-Form

Now that you have learned how to **accurately receive non-local messages**, the next section will cover:

✓ How to structure a **strong, well-formed non-local message.**

✓ The role of **emotional energy in amplifying transmission strength.**

✓ Techniques for **ensuring that the message reaches the intended recipient without distortion.**

Mastering the **sending process** completes the non-local cycle, allowing for **real-time, two-way communication** between the subconscious selves of sender and receiver.

Key Takeaways from This Section

💡 Non-local reception happens through images, emotions, and intuitive knowing—not words or logical thoughts.

💡 Trusting the first impression is essential—overthinking weakens accuracy.

💡 A relaxed, receptive state enhances subconscious communication—forcing a message blocks it.

💡 Recording impressions immediately prevents logical interference and strengthens subconscious confidence.

💡 The next step is learning how to send a non-local message with precision and power.

Section 7 – The Sending Process: How to Transmit a Clear Thought-Form

Now that you have learned how to **accurately receive non-local messages** (*see Section 6*), the next step is mastering **how to send thought-forms with precision and power.**

Non-local transmission follows the same principles as **thought-form projection for manifestation** (*see Chapter 3*), but instead of sending a thought-form to the **Transcendent Self**, you are sending it to the **subconscious self of another person** via the aka thread connection (*see Chapter 5*).

The clarity, strength, and **emotional charge** of the message determine how well it is received. A weak or scattered transmission will be difficult for the receiver's subconscious self to interpret, whereas a **focused, energy-charged message** will arrive with clarity and detail.

Step-by-Step Process for Sending a Non-local Message
To ensure your message is transmitted **accurately and powerfully**, follow this structured process:

1 Enter an Alpha State to Sharpen Focus

- Use **alpha induction techniques** (*see Chapter 4*) to calm the mind and prepare for transmission.

- Take **three deep breaths**, releasing any distractions or mental noise.

2 Activate the Aka Thread to the Recipient

- Mentally **visualize the aka thread** connecting you to the receiver.

- Affirm: *"I am now linking my subconscious self with [recipient's name] for clear communication."*

3 Structure the Thought-Form Before Sending

- Keep the message **simple and focused**—avoid overcomplicating it.

- If sending a word or phrase, **see it written in clear text** in your mind.

- If sending an image, **hold a strong, detailed mental picture of it.**

- If sending an emotion, **evoke that emotion within yourself first.**

✅ **Example Messages for Early Training:**
✓ A basic shape (e.g., a triangle, a circle).
✓ A color (e.g., blue, red).
✓ A single word (e.g., "light," "peace").
✓ A specific image (e.g., a tree, a mountain).

Start with **simple, distinct impressions** before progressing to **complex messages or abstract concepts.**

4 Charge the Thought-Form with Emotional Energy

- As covered in *Chapter 3*, emotions **amplify thought-forms** and make them more powerful.

- Feel a strong **intention and certainty** that the message is already received.

- The more **emotionally engaged** you are, the clearer the transmission.

✅ **Why This Works:**
✓ The subconscious self **responds strongly to emotional energy,** making the message stand out.
✓ A message that is **charged with certainty** is easier for the receiver to detect.
✓ **Doubt weakens the transmission**—send with full confidence.

5 Project the Thought-Form Along the Aka Thread

- **See the message travel along the aka thread** like a beam of light.

- Imagine the recipient's subconscious self **absorbing the message instantly**.

- Affirm: *"This message is now fully received by [recipient's name]."*

- Hold the focus for a few moments, then **let go**—do not mentally "chase" the message.

✅ **Why This Works:**
✓ Aka threads act as **instant transmission pathways**—the clearer the projection, the faster the message arrives.
✓ **Holding focus too long can create resistance**—send the message, then trust the process.

How to Know If Your Non-local Message Was Sent Successfully

After sending a message, you may experience:
✓ A **sudden sense of completion**—as if the message has "landed."
✓ A **mental release**, where your focus naturally shifts elsewhere.
✓ A **gut feeling or inner knowing** that the message was received.

If you feel **uncertain or disconnected**, the message may not have been strong enough. In this case:
✓ **Repeat the projection process with greater emotional charge.**
✓ **Simplify the message to make it clearer for the subconscious self.**
✓ **Ensure that you are in a fully relaxed state before attempting again.**

Common Mistakes and How to Avoid Them

✗ **Overthinking or forcing the message**

- **Mistake:** Trying too hard to "push" the message through conscious effort.

- **Solution:** Relax and **let the subconscious self do the work**—non-local communication happens effortlessly when properly aligned.

✗ Sending unfocused or cluttered messages

- **Mistake:** Mentally jumping between different images or words while transmitting.

- **Solution: Stick to one message at a time**—clarity ensures precision.

✗ Doubting the effectiveness of the transmission

- **Mistake:** Questioning whether the message was received.

- **Solution:** Once sent, **assume it was delivered and trust the process**—doubt weakens non-local confidence.

Strengthening Your Non-local Sending Ability
To refine and strengthen your ability to send clear, strong messages:

✓ **Practice daily with simple transmissions** before moving to complex thought-forms.
✓ **Use the energy-building techniques from Chapter 3** to increase transmission power.
✓ **Record your results in a non-local journal** to track accuracy and improvement.
✓ **Experiment with different partners and distances** to test effectiveness.

With repetition, the subconscious self becomes **naturally attuned** to sending messages, allowing for faster and more reliable non-local contact.

The Next Step: Perfecting Your Practice – Overcoming Challenges
Now that you have learned how to **send and receive non-local messages**, the next section will cover:
✓ How to troubleshoot **common non-local obstacles** (interference, weak reception, mental noise).
✓ Techniques for increasing **precision, speed, and long-distance**

non-local accuracy.

✓ How to refine subconscious communication for **instant, effortless non-local contact.**

Mastering these refinements ensures that non-local communication **becomes a predictable, consistent skill** rather than an occasional success.

Key Takeaways from This Section

💡 **Non-local messages must be structured clearly—start with simple impressions before advancing to complex thought-forms.**

💡 **Charging messages with emotional energy increases their strength and clarity.**

💡 **The aka thread acts as the subconscious transmission pathway—activating it ensures a direct, interference-free connection.**

💡 **Successful non-local sending feels effortless—forcing or doubting the process weakens the transmission.**

💡 **The next step is refining non-local accuracy and overcoming common challenges.**

Section 8 – Perfecting Your Practice: Overcoming Challenges

Now that you have developed the foundational skills of **sending and receiving non-local messages** (*see Sections 6 and 7*), the next step is refining your technique to ensure **consistency, accuracy, and reliability** in your non-local communication.

Even experienced practitioners encounter challenges such as **interference, weak reception, or inconsistent results**. However, these issues can be resolved with **focused adjustments** in energy management, mental conditioning, and subconscious alignment.

Common Non-local Challenges and How to Overcome Them
1 Weak or Unclear Messages

Symptoms:
✘ Messages feel faint or fragmented.
✘ The receiver reports only partial accuracy.
✘ Messages seem "distant" or slow to arrive.

Causes:
◈ Insufficient **energy charge** behind the message (*see Chapter 3 for energy-building techniques*).
◈ The thought-form is **not structured clearly** (*see Section 7 for message formation*).
◈ The sender or receiver is mentally **distracted or fatigued**.

Solutions:
✓ Perform **Lower Dan Tian energy charging** (*see Chapter 3*) before sending messages.
✓ **Simplify the message**—start with **single-word, image-based transmissions** before advancing to complex ideas.
✓ Ensure both sender and receiver are in **a relaxed alpha state** (*see Chapter 4 for induction techniques*).

---

2 Mental Interference and Overthinking

Symptoms:
✘ Doubting whether a received message is real or imagined.
✘ The logical mind tries to "fill in gaps" instead of accepting the first impression.
✘ Struggling to hold a clear image while sending.

Causes:
◈ The **conscious mind interferes** by analyzing and filtering subconscious impressions.
◈ A **lack of trust in the subconscious self** leads to second-guessing.
◈ The receiver expects a **literal word-for-word message**, rather than symbolic impressions.

Solutions:
✓ Accept the **first impression**—even if it seems random. The subconscious self communicates in **symbols, emotions, and sensory impressions** (*see Chapter 4*).
✓ Practice **automatic writing or sketching** received impressions before analyzing them—this bypasses mental interference.
✓ Develop a **daily practice of meditation and visualization** to improve subconscious communication.

✅ **Example Fix:**

- If you receive an image of a lion when the sender was thinking of "courage," **do not dismiss it**—the subconscious self often **translates non-local messages into symbols.**

---

3 Interference from External Energy Fields

Symptoms:
✗ Messages feel distorted or chaotic.
✗ Unwanted impressions or unrelated images appear.
✗ The connection feels unstable or disrupted.

Causes:
◈ Electromagnetic interference from **phones, Wi-Fi, or electronic devices**.
◈ Energetic disturbances from **strong emotions or external distractions**.
◈ Residual aka threads from **past energetic connections** diluting the transmission.

Solutions:
✓ **Practice in a low-tech environment**—turn off electronic devices during training sessions.
✓ **Cleanse your energy field** before each session using deep breathing or grounding techniques (*see Chapter 3*).
✓ **Strengthen the aka thread to the intended recipient** (*see Chapter 5*) to block interference from unrelated sources.

✅ Example Fix:

- If interference persists, visualize a **protective barrier of light** around you, allowing only the intended non-local message to pass through.

---

4 Inconsistent Results in Long-Distance Non-Local Communication

Symptoms:
✗ Success is high in close proximity but weak over long distances.
✗ Messages take longer to receive or are harder to interpret.
✗ The receiver gets vague impressions rather than clear messages.

Causes:
◈ The aka thread between sender and receiver is **not reinforced** for long-distance transmission.
◈ The subconscious self is **not fully trained to project beyond local space**.
◈ There is **insufficient energy behind the transmission**.

Solutions:
✔ Before sending a message, **charge the aka thread with energy** (*see Chapter 5*).
✔ Strengthen your ability to **extend awareness beyond physical location** by practicing **remote sensory projection** (*see Chapter 4*).
✔ Use a **stronger emotional charge** when sending the message to ensure clarity over long distances.

✅ Example Fix:

- If the message feels weak over distance, spend **extra time reinforcing the aka thread connection before sending.**

Refining Your Non-local Technique for Maximum Accuracy
Once the basic challenges are resolved, fine-tuning your non-local

ability will lead to **more precise, detailed, and real-time communication.**

1 Improving Speed and Efficiency

✓ **Use instant recall training**—practice sending and receiving messages with minimal delay to improve real-time response.
✓ **Avoid unnecessary repetition**—if the first impression is clear, trust it without re-confirming.
✓ **Train in different environments**—practice in both quiet and noisy settings to improve adaptability.

2 Strengthening Symbolic Interpretation

✓ **Maintain a non-local journal** to track patterns in received messages.
✓ **Practice dream interpretation techniques** to refine subconscious symbolism recognition.
✓ **Develop a shared symbolic language** with your non-local partner (e.g., agree on specific mental images for emotions like love, fear, or joy).

3 Testing Non-local Strength with Blind Trials

✓ Have a **third party randomly select symbols or words** for the sender to transmit.
✓ The receiver records impressions **without knowing the possible choices** to eliminate bias.
✓ Compare accuracy rates over multiple trials to track progress.

The Next Step: Expanding Non-local Abilities Over Distance

Now that you have refined **sending and receiving techniques**, the next section will explore:
✓ **How to project non-local messages across great distances with precision.**
✓ **Techniques for maintaining an active aka thread connection without energy loss.**

✓ How to use non-local contact for real-world applications such as intuitive decision-making.

Mastering long-distance non-local communication completes the training process, allowing for **instantaneous subconscious interaction, regardless of physical location.**

Key Takeaways from This Section

💡 **Common non-local challenges include weak transmissions, mental interference, external energy disruptions, and inconsistent long-distance results.**

💡 **Energy-building techniques, aka thread reinforcement, and subconscious trust eliminate most non-local obstacles.**

💡 **Fine-tuning your practice through instant recall training, symbolic interpretation, and blind trials strengthens accuracy.**

💡 **The next step is learning how to expand non-local contact over long distances with maximum clarity.**

Section 9 – Expanding Non-local Abilities Over Distance

Now that you have refined your **non-local sending and receiving techniques** (*see Sections 6-8*), the next step is **expanding your ability to communicate non-locally across great distances**.

Distance is not a limiting factor in non-local contact because **aka threads operate outside of space and time** (*see Chapter 5*). However, many people experience **weaker or delayed responses** when attempting long-distance non-local communication due to **insufficient energy, lack of focus, or subconscious self-doubt.**

This section will teach you how to **extend and reinforce the aka thread connection**, ensuring **instant, accurate, and interference-free** non-local communication across any distance.

Why Distance Does Not Affect Non-local Contact

Although traditional communication relies on physical signals (such as sound waves or electromagnetic frequencies), non-local contact works through **the subconscious network of aka threads**. These threads allow for:

✓ **Instantaneous connection** – Messages are transmitted at the speed of thought, with no delay.
✓ **Non-local interaction** – Aka threads exist beyond physical space, meaning non-local messages do not "travel" in a conventional sense.
✓ **Energetic persistence** – Once an aka thread is established, it remains intact unless deliberately severed.

However, while distance does not weaken the **thread itself, a sender's mental clarity, emotional charge, and subconscious confidence** determine the **strength of the transmission**.

Strengthening the Aka Thread for Long-Distance Communication

Before engaging in long-distance non-local contact, the aka thread must be **reinforced** to ensure a **stable and direct connection**.

Exercise: Long-Distance Aka Thread Charging

1 **nter a relaxed alpha state** (*see Chapter 4 for induction techniques*).
2 **Visualize the aka thread connecting you to the intended recipient.**
3 **Mentally "trace" the thread, following it from your subconscious self to the recipient's subconscious self.**
4 **Breathe deeply and send energy along the thread, reinforcing it with each exhale.**
5 **Affirm:** *"This connection is now fully open, clear, and strong, allowing instant communication."*
6 **Once the connection feels stable, proceed with sending the non-local message.**

✅ **Why This Works:**
✓ Strengthens the subconscious link, ensuring the recipient receives

197

the message clearly.

✓ Reinforces the non-local pathway, reducing signal loss or interference.

✓ Engages the subconscious self, keeping the channel **active and responsive**.

Adapting Non-local Transmission for Long-Distance Contact

To optimize long-distance non-local communication, adjust the **sending and receiving process** as follows:

✓ **Increase Emotional Charge** – Since non-local impressions can become **faint over distance**, amplify the energy behind the message by **feeling the thought-form intensely** (*see Chapter 3 for energy amplification techniques*).

✓ **Use a Strong Visual Anchor** – Instead of just thinking of the person's name, **visualize their face, voice, or a specific memory** to enhance subconscious recognition.

✓ **Reinforce Reception Timing** – Before sending the message, set a **clear expectation** for the receiver:

- *"You will receive this message the next time you enter a relaxed state."*

  ✓ **Repeat the Transmission if Necessary** – If unsure whether the message was received, **send it a second time** with greater intensity.

Testing Accuracy in Long-Distance Non-Local Communication

To measure the effectiveness of long-distance non-local contact, perform structured accuracy tests:

Blind Non-local Sending Trials

✓ Have a sender select **a random object, word, or image** and transmit it to the receiver.

✓ The receiver **records their impressions** without knowing the

possible choices.
✓ Compare results over multiple trials to track accuracy.

Pre-Scheduled Non-local Messages

✓ The sender **chooses a time to send a message**, noting the exact time of transmission.
✓ The receiver **records impressions at the moment they feel an incoming message** (without prior knowledge of when it was sent).
✓ Compare timestamps to determine **if the message was received synchronously**.

✅ **Why This Works:**
✓ Eliminates **bias and guesswork**, allowing for **objective validation** of non-local ability.
✓ Strengthens the subconscious self's ability to **send and receive at precise times**.
✓ Builds confidence in **long-distance accuracy**, leading to faster, clearer results.

Overcoming Long-Distance Non-local Obstacles
Despite strong aka threads, some people struggle with long-distance non-local communication due to **subconscious resistance, emotional interference, or environmental factors.**

1 Lack of Immediate Feedback Creates Doubt

◈ **Issue:** Unlike in-person non-local contact, long-distance communication does not always provide immediate confirmation.
◈ **Solution:** Assume the message was received and **avoid dwelling on uncertainty**—doubt weakens future transmissions.

2 The Receiver Is Not in a Receptive State

◈ **Issue:** If the receiver is mentally distracted, they may not consciously register the message.
◈ **Solution:** Set an expectation that the receiver will receive the

message **in their next relaxed state** (e.g., before sleep, during meditation).

3 Non-local Signals Get Lost in Background Noise

◈ **Issue:** The receiver picks up **unrelated impressions** or experiences mental interference.
◈ **Solution:** Reinforce the aka thread before sending and use **strong emotional energy** to differentiate the message from subconscious clutter.

✅ **Example Fix:**

- If the receiver reports **mixed impressions, repeat the transmission with greater intensity** and ensure both parties are **mentally prepared before the session.**

Finalizing Long-Distance Non-local Mastery
With consistent training, long-distance non-local ability becomes:
✓ **Instantaneous** – Messages arrive without delay or distortion.
✓ **Effortless** – Sending and receiving happen naturally, without conscious effort.
✓ **Accurate** – Thought-forms are interpreted clearly, without misinterpretation.

Once you can **reliably communicate non-locally over any distance**, you are ready to explore the **real-world applications of non-local mastery**—the final step in subconscious communication training.

The Next Step: The Real-World Applications of Non-local Contact
Now that you have established a **strong, reliable non-local connection across any distance**, the next section will focus on:
✓ How to use non-local contact for **intuition, guidance, and decision-making.**

✓ How to apply subconscious communication in **everyday life, relationships, and professional settings**.
✓ The ethical considerations of using non-local abilities responsibly.

Mastering these applications allows you to integrate **non-local awareness into daily life**, unlocking the full potential of the subconscious self.

Key Takeaways from This Section
💡 **Long-distance non-local communication is possible because aka threads operate beyond physical space and time.**
💡 **Reinforcing the aka thread before sending a message strengthens long-distance accuracy.**
💡 **Using strong emotional charge, visual anchors, and precise timing improves transmission success.**
💡 **Testing non-local accuracy through structured trials ensures objective validation of results.**
💡 **The next step is applying non-local skills to real-world situations for guidance, intuition, and deeper subconscious awareness.**

Section 10 – The Real-World Applications of Non-local Contact

Now that you have developed the ability to **send and receive non-local messages over any distance** (*see Section 9*), the next step is learning how to apply **subconscious communication in everyday life**.

Non-local contact is not just a skill for controlled practice sessions—it has **practical uses in relationships, decision-making, intuitive guidance, and professional interactions**. The subconscious self is always engaged in **non-verbal, energetic exchanges with others**, whether you are aware of it or not. By mastering non-local awareness, you can **enhance connection, strengthen intuition, and navigate life with greater clarity and insight.**

How Non-local Contact Enhances Daily Life

The subconscious self is constantly **picking up on subtle impressions from others**, even when no words are spoken. By developing **intentional non-local awareness**, you can:

✓ **Deepen relationships** by sensing emotions, thoughts, and unspoken needs.
✓ **Improve professional interactions** by understanding what is not being said.
✓ **Enhance intuitive decision-making** by tapping into the subconscious field of collective knowledge.

Even if you do not **deliberately engage in non-local communication**, the ability to recognize and interpret **incoming subconscious impressions** will give you a significant advantage in understanding people, situations, and opportunities.

---

1 Strengthening Relationships Through Non-local Awareness

Non-local connection naturally enhances relationships by allowing for **deeper emotional resonance and mutual understanding**.

Signs of Spontaneous Non-local Connection in Relationships:

✓ Thinking about someone moments before they call or text.
✓ Instantly sensing a loved one's emotional state without verbal cues.
✓ Feeling an energetic pull toward someone before meeting them.

By training **intentional non-local contact**, you can:
✓ **Strengthen the aka thread connection** between you and loved ones (*see Chapter 5*).
✓ **Increase emotional attunement** by sensing feelings before they are expressed.

✓ **Enhance communication and conflict resolution** by understanding unspoken concerns.

☑ **Practical Exercise for Relationship Non-Local Communication:**
1 **Before speaking with someone, enter a relaxed alpha state** (*see Chapter 4*).
2 **Mentally tune into their energy field**—what emotions, thoughts, or impressions arise?
3 **After your interaction, compare your impressions** with what was actually discussed.
4 **Refine accuracy over time by noticing patterns in subconscious reception.**

---

2 Using Non-local Awareness for Professional and Social Situations

Non-local contact can be a powerful tool in **business, leadership, and negotiations**, allowing you to:
✓ Sense **hidden motives or unspoken concerns** in meetings.
✓ Gauge the **energy of a room** before speaking or making decisions.
✓ Strengthen **team cohesion** by establishing a deeper energetic connection with colleagues.

☑ **Practical Exercise for Business and Social Non-local Awareness:**
1 **Before a meeting or interaction, enter a receptive state** and mentally "scan" the room's energy.
2 **Observe first impressions**—who feels open, who seems hesitant, and what energetic dynamics are present?
3 **Notice how your subconscious impressions align with spoken words**—do they match, or is something unspoken?
4 **Use this awareness to adjust your communication strategy**, ensuring stronger connections and better outcomes.

---

3 Non-local Guidance for Decision-Making and Intuition

Since the subconscious self **connects to the greater field of information**, non-local awareness can be used to:
✓ Receive **insight about future outcomes** before they unfold.
✓ Strengthen **inner guidance** by tuning into subconscious wisdom.
✓ Sense **opportunities and risks** before taking action.

✅ **Practical Exercise for Non-local Decision-Making:**
1 **Enter a meditative state and focus on a decision you need to make.**
2 **Ask your subconscious self for insight**—visualize receiving a non-local message related to the outcome.
3 **Observe the first impressions that arise** (images, emotions, or direct knowing).
4 **Compare these impressions with actual outcomes over time**, refining subconscious accuracy.

With practice, your **subconscious self will begin providing non-local insight naturally**, allowing for effortless intuitive decision-making.

Ethical Considerations of Non-local Contact
With increased non-local awareness comes a greater responsibility to **use this skill ethically**. Non-local contact should be used **to enhance connection, improve understanding, and support the well-being of others**, never as a means of control or manipulation.

✓ **Respect privacy**—non-local impressions should never be forced or used invasively.
✓ **Only engage in non-local contact with mutual agreement**—for structured practice, both participants should be willing and aware.
✓ **Use non-local insight to uplift and empower** rather than to influence or deceive.

The subconscious self is most **effective and responsive** when non-local skills are used with **integrity, clarity, and benevolent intent**.

Finalizing Your Non-local Mastery
With regular practice, non-local contact will become:
✓ **Effortless** – Your subconscious self will automatically sense, interpret, and respond to non-local impressions.
✓ **Practical** – You will integrate subconscious awareness into daily life, improving relationships, intuition, and decision-making.
✓ **Reliable** – Non-local accuracy will improve, allowing you to confidently interpret subconscious messages.

However, even with developed non-local skills, emotional blockages, unresolved subconscious patterns, and limiting beliefs can still interfere with clarity. The next chapter introduces tools for clearing these blockages, including the Personal Demon Demolisher, which allows you to eliminate subconscious resistance and ensure that your non-local practice remains pure, precise, and interference-free.

By resolving these internal barriers, you will unlock the full potential of non-local mastery, ensuring that nothing stands in the way of your ability to communicate clearly, accurately, and powerfully through the subconscious self.

Key Takeaways from This Section
💡 **Non-local awareness enhances relationships, business interactions, and intuitive decision-making.**
💡 **Strengthening the aka thread improves emotional attunement and communication with loved ones.**
💡 **Subconscious non-local insights can provide guidance for major decisions.**
💡 **Ethical non-local practice requires respect, integrity, and mutual consent.**
💡 **Even with strong non-local abilities, emotional blockages can still interfere—next, you will learn tools to clear them.**

Chapter 7: Tools For Clearing Blockages

Section 1 – Identifying the Hidden Barriers to Success

If you are not experiencing the success, happiness, health, relationships, or financial abundance that you desire, the problem isn't external circumstances—it's subconscious programming. This programming, which operates beneath conscious awareness, determines what you believe is possible and what you unconsciously resist.

The subconscious self is not actively blocking you from achieving your goals. Instead, it is simply executing the instructions it has been conditioned to follow. If deep-seated beliefs contradict your conscious desires, you will experience internal conflict that manifests as hesitation, fear, procrastination, or self-doubt.

The first step in clearing these barriers is understanding how they were formed in the first place.

Subconscious Conditioning from Childhood

From infancy through adolescence, the subconscious self is in a highly suggestible state. During this period, it absorbs beliefs, behaviors, and expectations from:

- Parents and caregivers – shaping core beliefs about love, worthiness, and success.

- Teachers and authority figures – instilling perceptions of intelligence, discipline, and societal expectations.

- Media and culture – reinforcing ideas about money, relationships, and self-image.

- Religious and social structures – defining morality, values, and purpose.

These early messages form the foundation of your subconscious programming, even if you no longer consciously agree with them.

"Everything we experience from birth onward, whether positive or negative, gets recorded into our subconscious self. Because of this, the beliefs, fears, limitations, and emotional patterns we absorbed from our family, culture, and past experiences shape the way we think and act today—often without us realizing it."

This means that if you grew up hearing statements like:
✓ "Money doesn't grow on trees."
✓ "You have to work hard just to get by."
✓ "People like us don't get ahead in life."

...then your subconscious self accepts these as absolute truths and organizes your actions accordingly.

These beliefs create an internal set point, much like a thermostat. If you attempt to exceed your pre-programmed limits of success, love, or abundance, the subconscious self will pull you back to what feels "safe"—even if that means staying stuck in struggle, lack, or dissatisfaction.

Common Limiting Beliefs That Shape Reality
Limiting beliefs operate in the background of your subconscious, quietly influencing every decision you make. The most common examples include:

1. "I'm not good enough."

   o   This belief leads to self-doubt, hesitation, and undervaluing your abilities.

2. "I don't deserve it."

   o   If this belief is active, success feels uncomfortable, and self-sabotage becomes inevitable.

3. "I'm not lucky/smart/wealthy enough."

- The subconscious self filters out opportunities that contradict this self-concept.

4. "People like me don't succeed."

    - This belief stems from generational conditioning and can create a deep-seated resistance to breaking free from perceived limitations.

These thought patterns run continuously, like an internal dialogue that frames how you interpret the world. Because they have been repeated thousands of times, they feel like objective truth rather than subconscious programming.

The Power of Automatic Thought Loops

Limiting beliefs become self-perpetuating cycles in the subconscious self.

- A negative belief creates a reinforcing emotional response.

- That emotion strengthens the belief, making it feel even more real.

- Over time, the belief hardens into an unquestioned reality, guiding thoughts and behaviors without conscious awareness.

For example:

- If you believe "I never have enough money," your subconscious self will:

    - Filter out opportunities that could lead to wealth.

    - Reinforce financial stress through emotional reactions.

    - Maintain circumstances that validate the belief.

"What you unconsciously expect, you unconsciously create. If your subconscious self believes struggle is necessary, you will continue to experience struggle—no matter how much conscious effort you apply to change your situation."

This explains why willpower alone is not enough to override deeply ingrained beliefs. Unless these automatic thought loops are consciously identified and reprogrammed, they will continue to shape reality, keeping you stuck in the same patterns.

The Key to Change: Becoming Aware of Your Subconscious Patterns
The first step in clearing internal barriers is bringing subconscious patterns into conscious awareness.

✓ **Pay attention to recurring negative emotions—they are signals of underlying subconscious beliefs.**
✓ **Notice moments of hesitation, doubt, or fear—they indicate inner resistance to your desired outcomes.**
✓ **Observe your automatic reactions to success, abundance, and happiness—are they met with excitement or discomfort?**

By shining a light on hidden thought loops, you gain the power to break free from unconscious limitations and rewire the subconscious self for success.

In the next section, we will explore how your emotions serve as a mirror to your subconscious programming and how to use them as a tool for transformation.

Key Takeaways from Section 1
💡 Your subconscious programming, not external circumstances, is the real barrier to success.
💡 Limiting beliefs are absorbed from childhood and operate beneath conscious awareness.
💡 Negative thought loops create reinforcing emotional spirals, making them feel like absolute truth.
💡 Bringing these patterns into conscious awareness is the first step toward reprogramming the subconscious self.

Section 2 – How Your Feelings Reveal Your Subconscious Programming

Your emotions are more than just fleeting reactions to external events—they are **direct indicators of your subconscious programming**. The subconscious self does not use language the way the conscious self does; instead, it **communicates through emotions, imagery, and impulses**.

This means that every **persistent emotional state** you experience is a reflection of an **underlying belief or thought-pattern** stored in your subconscious self.

If you want to know **what your subconscious self truly believes**, pay attention to how you feel **when you think about your goals, dreams, and desires**.

The Emotional Feedback Loop

Every thought you have **creates a corresponding emotional response**. This emotional charge then **reinforces the thought**, creating a feedback loop that strengthens **whatever belief is dominant in the subconscious self**.

Negative Thought-Emotion Spiral

- You think: **"I never have enough money."**

- This thought triggers feelings of **anxiety, frustration, or hopelessness**.

- These emotions **reinforce the belief** that financial struggle is your reality.

- The belief causes you to **notice and attract more evidence** that supports it.

- The cycle **continues** until the subconscious self accepts it as an unchangeable truth.

Positive Thought-Emotion Spiral

- You think: **"I am on the path to financial freedom."**

- This thought generates feelings of **optimism, motivation, and confidence**.

- These emotions **strengthen the belief** that abundance is possible for you.

- The belief causes you to **take inspired action and recognize new opportunities**.

- The cycle **reinforces itself**, moving you toward success.

"Your subconscious self does not determine what is true or false. It simply reinforces whatever you focus on most consistently."

This explains why **repeated emotional states shape reality**—your subconscious self actively **seeks out experiences, people, and circumstances that validate your dominant emotional frequency**.

Using Emotions as a Diagnostic Tool

Your emotions act as a **real-time diagnostic tool** for identifying subconscious resistance. If you experience **fear, doubt, or anxiety** when thinking about a goal, it means that your subconscious self is holding **a contradictory belief**.

For example, if you dream of financial freedom but feel:

✔ **Excitement and confidence** → Your subconscious self supports this outcome.
✔ **Unease, fear, or skepticism** → Your subconscious self is programmed with **contradictory beliefs** about money.

This emotional feedback provides **a precise roadmap** for uncovering subconscious limitations.

"If you want to know what your subconscious self believes about success, relationships, or abundance, simply observe how you feel when you think about those things."

Instead of **fighting negative emotions**, use them as **a guide to uncover hidden programming**.

Identifying Hidden Subconscious Blocks

To reprogram the subconscious self, you must first **identify and acknowledge the thought-patterns that are generating resistance**. The following steps will help:

1. **Notice Emotional Reactions to Success-Based Thoughts**

   o   Think about your biggest goals.

   o   Observe your **instant** emotional response.

If you feel discomfort, hesitation, or fear, this is your subconscious self signaling resistance.

2. **Pay Attention to Recurring Negative Emotions**

   o   Do you frequently feel unworthy, anxious, or stuck?

   o   What circumstances trigger these emotions most often?

Your most persistent emotional states are tied to subconscious programming.

3. **Look for Emotional 'Drop-Offs'**

   o   If you feel **excitement about a goal but then suddenly feel doubt or fear**, this is a sign of **conflicting subconscious beliefs**.

   o   Example: You feel excited about the idea of being financially free, but then a voice inside says, "That's not realistic."

These emotional drop-offs indicate the presence of subconscious blocks that need to be cleared.

Why You Can't Outthink Emotional Programming

One of the biggest mistakes people make when trying to change their reality is **relying on willpower alone**.

Willpower operates at the **conscious level**, but deep-rooted beliefs exist at the **subconscious level**. If your subconscious self holds a belief that contradicts your conscious goal, emotional resistance will **override your willpower every time**.

For example:

- If you say: **"I am wealthy"** but feel anxiety about money, your subconscious self will **reject the affirmation** because it contradicts your dominant emotional state.

- If you try to push forward while ignoring emotional misalignment, you will experience **frustration, burnout, or self-sabotage**.

This is why **affirmations alone do not work unless they are paired with emotional alignment**.

"The subconscious self responds to emotion, not logic. If your emotions contradict your conscious goals, the subconscious will default to the stronger emotional signal."

To change subconscious programming, you must **first change the emotional associations linked to your desires**.

2.5 Rewriting Emotional Associations for Success

The fastest way to shift subconscious programming is to **intentionally generate the emotions that match your desired reality**.

Step 1: Identify the Emotional State of Your Goal

- If your goal is financial abundance, what does **wealth feel like** to you?

- If your goal is love, what does **deep connection feel like**?

- If your goal is success, what does **confidence and achievement feel like**?

Step 2: Generate That Feeling Now

- Use **visualization** (*see Chapter 3 on Multi-Sensory Thought-Forms*).

- Recall **past experiences** where you felt this way.

- Engage in **activities that naturally evoke that emotion**.

By **aligning your emotional state with your goal**, you **retrain your subconscious self to accept it as your new normal**.

The Next Step: Transforming Emotional Resistance into Support
Now that you understand how emotions reflect subconscious programming, the next section will explore:

✓ **How to transform subconscious resistance into alignment.**
✓ **Why "self-sabotage" is actually just subconscious protection.**
✓ **How to clear emotional roadblocks to success.**

By learning to **neutralize emotional resistance**, you can **train the subconscious self to fully support your desires—without internal struggle or doubt.**

Key Takeaways from Section 2
💡 **Your emotions are a mirror of your subconscious programming.**
💡 **Negative emotional responses signal limiting subconscious**

beliefs.

💡 Persistent thought-emotion loops shape your reality.

💡 You cannot outthink emotional resistance—you must align with the feeling of success.

💡 The next step is learning how to transform emotional resistance into subconscious alignment.

Section 3 – There Is No Such Thing as Self-Sabotage

Many people believe that they **sabotage themselves** when they fail to take action, procrastinate, or fall back into old patterns. But what if **self-sabotage doesn't actually exist?**

The truth is, the subconscious self is **always working in your best interest**—it just doesn't always define "best" in the way the conscious self does. If your subconscious programming contradicts your conscious goals, your subconscious self will act in **alignment with its dominant programming, not your conscious desires**.

This is why it may feel like you are **blocked, stuck, or even working against yourself**. But you are not sabotaging yourself—you are simply **following subconscious instructions that were set in place long ago**.

The Subconscious Self Always Says "Yes"

Your subconscious self **never works against you**. It is **not actively trying to keep you from success, love, health, or abundance**—it is simply responding to the dominant input it has received throughout your life.

✓ If your subconscious programming says **"Success is dangerous,"** it will guide you toward safety—**which may mean avoiding success**.
✓ If it believes **"Wealth is stressful,"** it will steer you away from financial abundance.

216

✓ If it holds **"Love leads to pain,"** it will prevent deep relationships from forming.

"You are not sabotaging yourself. You are just following subconscious instructions that were programmed into you long ago."

When subconscious resistance arises, **it's not self-sabotage—it's self-protection**. The subconscious self is **acting out the instructions it believes will keep you safe, based on the experiences and beliefs you absorbed earlier in life**.

Why the Subconscious Resists Change
To the subconscious self, **change equals uncertainty**. And uncertainty triggers **an automatic safety response**.

The subconscious self **prioritizes safety and stability** above all else, even if that means **keeping you in circumstances that feel unsatisfying or limiting**.

- If you grew up in an environment where struggle was the norm, your subconscious self will **resist ease and abundance** because they feel unfamiliar.

- If you have always associated hard work with self-worth, your subconscious self will **reject effortless success** because it contradicts your identity.

- If relationships in the past have led to pain, your subconscious self may **avoid deep emotional connection** to protect you from being hurt again.

This is not sabotage—it is the subconscious **doing its job of keeping you in familiar, predictable territory**.

"The subconscious self is wired for survival, not happiness. If success, wealth, or love feel unsafe, your subconscious self will resist them—until it is retrained to accept them as safe and normal."

The Role of Resistance in the Change Process

Dr. Carl Jung famously said, **"What you resist not only persists, but grows in size."**

This is exactly how subconscious resistance works. The more you **struggle against** your own subconscious programming, the more energy you give it.

- If you **fight against procrastination**, it becomes stronger.
- If you **judge yourself for feeling fear**, the fear grows.
- If you **obsess over why success feels difficult**, you reinforce the difficulty.

The key to overcoming subconscious resistance is not fighting it— it is understanding it.

Instead of asking, **"Why do I sabotage myself?"** ask:
✓ *"What is my subconscious trying to protect me from?"*
✓ *"What belief is keeping me in this pattern?"*
✓ *"How can I show my subconscious self that this change is safe?"*

When you stop **judging resistance** and start **working with it**, you create the opportunity for deep, lasting transformation.

How to Reprogram the Subconscious to Say "Yes" to What You Desire

The subconscious self does not resist change **because it wants to keep you stuck**—it resists because it doesn't have **proof** that the new outcome is safe.

The solution? **Provide evidence that success, wealth, love, or health are safe and desirable.**

Step 1: Identify the Subconscious "No"

- What goal do you struggle to achieve?

- When you imagine having it, what negative emotions or doubts arise?

- These reactions reveal where the subconscious is saying, **"No, that doesn't feel safe."**

Step 2: Shift the Emotional Association

- Instead of **pushing harder**, ask yourself:

  o *"What would make this feel safe?"*

  o *"What evidence can I find that supports this change?"*

- Find small, real-life examples that **contradict the limiting belief**.

- **Example:** If your subconscious believes **"Money is stressful,"** start looking for people who handle money with ease and joy.

Step 3: Train the Subconscious with Repetition and Emotion

- The subconscious self learns through **repetition and strong emotions**.

- Use **multi-sensory thought-forms** (*see Chapter 3*) to visualize success **while feeling deeply safe and excited about it**.

- The stronger the emotional imprint, the faster the subconscious will accept it as truth.

By **shifting subconscious associations**, you move from **resistance to alignment**, allowing success, love, and abundance to manifest without internal conflict.

The Next Step: Reprogramming Limiting Language
Now that we've explored how subconscious resistance is actually self-protection, the next section will dive into:

✓ How **language** affects subconscious programming.
✓ Why words like **"don't" and "can't"** reinforce the very patterns you

want to change.

✓ How to **speak in a way that aligns with your subconscious self's natural programming**.

When you change how you **speak to yourself and about yourself**, you change what your subconscious self accepts as reality.

Key Takeaways from Section 3

💡 There is no such thing as self-sabotage—only subconscious self-protection.

💡 Your subconscious self always says "yes" to its dominant programming.

💡 If success, love, or wealth feel unsafe, the subconscious self will resist them.

💡 The key to change is showing your subconscious self that new outcomes are safe.

💡 The next step is learning how to reprogram subconscious beliefs through language.

Section 4 – Why It Is So Important to Avoid Words Like "Don't"

One of the most overlooked but powerful influences on subconscious programming is **language**. The subconscious self is highly **literal** and does not process negatives in the same way the conscious mind does. This means that words like **"don't," "can't," and "won't"** often reinforce the very patterns you want to change.

Understanding how to **communicate effectively with your subconscious self** is crucial for reprogramming limiting beliefs and achieving success with greater ease.

How the Subconscious Self Interprets Language
The subconscious self does not analyze language the way the conscious self does. Instead, it processes **images, emotions, and direct commands**.

This means that when you say something like:

- **"I don't want to get sick."**

- **"I can't afford to fail."**

- **"I won't mess this up."**

Your subconscious self focuses on **the primary subject of the statement**—not the negation.

✓ **"I don't want to get sick"** → The subconscious registers **"Get sick."**
✓ **"I can't afford to fail"** → The subconscious hears **"Fail."**
✓ **"I won't mess this up"** → The subconscious locks onto **"Mess this up."**

"The subconscious self does not recognize 'don't' or 'can't.' It only registers the core idea that follows the negation."

This is why people who **focus on what they don't want** often experience **more of those very things**.

The Self-Fulfilling Prophecy of Negative Language
Because the subconscious self takes instructions literally, using **negative phrasing** strengthens undesired outcomes rather than preventing them.

For example, imagine two people preparing for an important meeting:

1. **Person A says:**

    o   "I don't want to mess up."

    o   "I can't forget what I need to say."

- "I won't let my nerves get the best of me."

The subconscious self **focuses on 'mess up,' 'forget,' and 'nerves'**, reinforcing anxiety.

2. **Person B says:**

    - "I am confident and well-prepared."

    - "I remember everything with ease."

    - "I feel calm and in control."

The subconscious self **locks onto 'confident,' 'remember,' and 'calm,'** strengthening success.

Even though Person A and Person B have the **same goal**, Person A is unconsciously **programming failure** while Person B is reinforcing **success**.

"Your subconscious self is always listening—make sure it hears what you actually want, not what you fear."

The Power of Reframing Language for Success
To align subconscious programming with success, it is essential to **replace negative statements with positive, outcome-focused language**.

Negative Statement (Weakens Subconscious Alignment)	Reframed Statement (Strengthens Subconscious Alignment)
"I don't want to be late."	"I arrive on time with ease."
"I can't fail at this."	"I succeed with confidence."
"I won't let fear control me."	"I move forward with courage."

Negative Statement (Weakens Subconscious Alignment)	Reframed Statement (Strengthens Subconscious Alignment)
"I need to stop procrastinating."	"I take action easily and effortlessly."

This simple shift in **wording** creates a profound impact on **subconscious receptivity**.

By **focusing on what you do want instead of what you don't want**, you direct the subconscious self toward success rather than reinforcing struggle.

Why Emotionally Charged Words Strengthen Subconscious Programming

Language alone is powerful, but when paired with **strong emotions**, subconscious programming accelerates dramatically.

- **Words with fear, worry, or stress attached** reinforce negative patterns more deeply.

- **Words with confidence, joy, and enthusiasm** anchor positive outcomes more firmly.

This is why it is **critical to not only reframe language but to reinforce it with elevated emotions**.

For example, instead of saying:
✓ **"I hope I succeed"** (which implies uncertainty)...
✓ Say: **"I am certain of my success"** while feeling deep confidence and excitement.

"Emotion is the glue that makes subconscious programming stick. The stronger the emotional charge, the faster the subconscious accepts the new belief."

To make a new belief **take root quickly**, say it with **conviction, certainty, and enthusiasm**.

Practical Exercise: Reprogramming Language Patterns
Step 1: Identify Common Negative Statements You Use

- Notice the words you use when talking about challenges, goals, and fears.

- Write them down exactly as you say them.

Step 2: Reframe Each Statement into Positive, Outcome-Focused Language

- Convert each negative statement into one that aligns with what you actually want.

- Ensure it focuses on **the desired outcome, not avoidance of failure.**

Step 3: Attach a Strong Positive Emotion to the New Statement

- Say it **with confidence and certainty**.

- Visualize yourself **living the new reality with excitement and ease**.

Example Transformation:

Original Statement	Reframed Statement with Emotion
"I don't want to be alone."	"I am attracting deep, meaningful relationships with ease."
"I can't afford to fail."	"I succeed effortlessly in all that I do."
"I won't let my fears hold me back."	"I move forward with confidence and excitement."

By repeating **reframed statements** consistently, with **strong emotion**, you condition the subconscious self to accept them as **new reality**.

The Next Step: Mastering Emotional Influence
Now that we have explored the **impact of language on subconscious programming**, the next section will focus on:

✓ How **emotions** shape reality even more powerfully than words.
✓ Why **negative emotions act as barriers to success**.
✓ How to **intentionally shift your emotional state to align with success, wealth, and happiness**.

When you combine **conscious language shifts with emotional mastery**, you gain full control over **how your subconscious self creates your reality**.

Key Takeaways from Section 4
💡 **The subconscious self does not process negative words like "don't" or "can't."**
💡 **Negative language reinforces the very patterns you are trying to change.**
💡 **Shifting statements to focus on the desired outcome reprograms the subconscious for success.**
💡 **Attaching strong emotions to affirmations accelerates subconscious acceptance.**
💡 **The next step is learning how emotions shape reality and how to harness them for transformation.**

Section 5 – Feelings Are Powerful Forces in Reality Creation

Your emotions are not just reactions to external circumstances—they are **active forces that shape your reality**. The subconscious self **does not distinguish between real and imagined emotions**; it simply **amplifies whatever emotional frequency is dominant** and attracts experiences that match it.

If you have ever noticed that negative emotions seem to **spiral and intensify**, while positive emotions **lead to synchronicities and success**, this is because emotions serve as **the fuel for subconscious programming**.

By learning how to **intentionally generate and sustain high-vibration emotions**, you gain the ability to **align with success, abundance, and fulfillment effortlessly**.

Your Reality Is a Mirror of Your Emotional State
Every emotion carries a specific energetic frequency. This frequency determines what you attract and experience in life.

✓ **Elevated emotions (gratitude, joy, excitement, confidence)** → Attract success, opportunity, and synchronicities.
✓ **Low-vibration emotions (fear, frustration, guilt, anxiety)** → Reinforce struggle, obstacles, and stagnation.

The subconscious self **does not analyze whether an emotion is helpful or harmful**—it simply **reinforces whatever you focus on most intensely**.

"The universe does not give you what you want—it gives you what you are emotionally aligned with."

If you habitually feel:
✓ **Worry about money** → You reinforce scarcity.
✓ **Doubt about success** → You reinforce failure.
✓ **Confidence in your abilities** → You reinforce achievement.

This is why shifting **emotional states** is **the fastest way to change reality**.

Emotions Are Like Warning Lights on a Car Dashboard
Negative emotions are **not the enemy**—they are **signals from your subconscious self**.

Imagine the warning lights on a car dashboard:
✓ If the **oil light** turns on, it's not an attack—it's an **indicator that something needs attention**.
✓ If the **gas light** comes on, the solution is **not to get angry at the dashboard**—it's to **refuel the car**.

Negative emotions work the same way.

- **Fear, worry, or anxiety** signal that **a subconscious belief is contradicting your conscious goal**.

- **Guilt or shame** indicate **self-judgment or unprocessed emotional blocks**.

- **Frustration or anger** point to **internal conflict or resistance to change**.

Instead of fighting negative emotions, **use them as a tool to identify limiting subconscious patterns**.

"Negative emotions don't mean you're failing—they mean your subconscious self is revealing what needs to be reprogrammed."

The Subconscious Learns Through Emotion, Not Logic
One of the biggest misconceptions about manifestation and subconscious programming is the belief that **thoughts alone create reality**.

While thoughts are important, **it is the emotional charge behind them that determines whether they take root**.

227

- If you say, **"I am successful,"** but feel doubt → The subconscious self rejects the thought.

- If you say, **"I am successful,"** and feel excitement → The subconscious self accepts the thought as truth.

This is why **affirmations and visualization only work if they are paired with strong emotional energy**.

"The subconscious self does not respond to logic—it responds to the emotional charge behind your thoughts."

To **reprogram reality**, you must **generate the feelings of your desired outcome before it arrives**.

How to Intentionally Shift Your Emotional State

If emotions are the fuel for subconscious programming, then learning to **control your emotional state** gives you full influence over your reality.

Here's how to do it:

Step 1: Identify the Emotional Frequency of Your Desired Outcome

- If you want **financial freedom**, what does it **feel** like?

- If you want **deep love**, what does it **feel** like?

- If you want **success**, what does it **feel** like?

Your subconscious self **needs to experience the emotion now** before it will bring it into reality.

Step 2: Generate That Emotion Now

You don't have to wait for external success to **feel successful**. You can generate the feeling **internally first**, which signals to the subconscious self that this state is normal.

228

Ways to generate **desired emotions instantly**:
✓ **Visualization** – Imagine yourself already living your desired outcome.
✓ **Gratitude** – Focus on what you already have that matches your goal.
✓ **Movement** – Physical activity shifts emotional states rapidly.
✓ **Music** – Listening to music that evokes success, joy, or love.

The **stronger the emotional intensity**, the faster the subconscious self **accepts it as reality**.

The Next Step: Clearing Negative Emotional Blocks
Now that you understand how emotions shape reality, the next section will introduce:

✓ **Why clearing negative emotions is essential before creating new ones.**
✓ **The two most powerful methods for emotional clearing.**
✓ **How to dissolve subconscious resistance and align with high-vibration emotions.**

By **removing the emotional blocks that contradict success**, you allow the subconscious self to fully support your highest potential.

Key Takeaways from Section 5
💡 **Your emotions create your reality, not just your thoughts.**
💡 **Negative emotions are not enemies—they are signals revealing subconscious patterns.**
💡 **The subconscious self responds to emotional energy, not logic.**
💡 **Generating the feeling of success before it happens accelerates manifestation.**
💡 **The next step is clearing emotional resistance to fully align with success.**

Section 6 – Two Powerful Methods for Clearing Non-Resourceful Feelings

Now that we understand that emotions shape reality, the next step is learning how to **clear negative emotional patterns** that block success. Many people attempt to create positive emotions without addressing the **underlying emotional resistance**, which is like trying to plant flowers in rocky soil—**the old emotional patterns must be removed first**.

Clearing negative emotions is **not about ignoring them** or pretending they don't exist. It's about **acknowledging, neutralizing, and replacing them with powerful, aligned emotions** that support your success.

Why Clearing Work Is Necessary Before Installing New Emotional Patterns

Imagine you visit a dentist because of a painful cavity. Would you ask the dentist to **simply place a filling over the decay** without first cleaning out the damaged area? Of course not. The decay **must be removed first**, or the problem will continue to spread beneath the surface.

The same principle applies to subconscious programming. **If old emotional patterns are not cleared, they will continue to operate in the background, sabotaging new beliefs.**

This is why many people experience **temporary success** with affirmations, visualization, or goal-setting but eventually revert back to their old patterns. The **root emotional imprints were never addressed**, so the subconscious self **defaults to the original programming**.

To ensure that **new, empowering emotional patterns take root**, we must first **clear the non-resourceful emotions that are contradicting them**.

There are many methods for emotional clearing, but two of the **most effective and time-tested techniques** are:

1. **The Personal Demon Demolisher** – A powerful process that neutralizes subconscious resistance using energy-based techniques.

2. **Ho'oponopono** – A Hawaiian reconciliation and clearing method that dissolves emotional blocks at their root.

Both techniques work by **releasing stored emotional patterns from the subconscious self**, allowing for **rapid transformation and alignment with success**.

The Personal Demon Demolisher: Clearing Deep-Rooted Emotional Patterns
The **Personal Demon Demolisher** is designed to **eliminate subconscious resistance, self-sabotage, and emotional triggers** that block success. It works by addressing **deep-seated limiting beliefs** and **neutralizing the emotional charge attached to them**.

Step 1: Identifying the "Personal Demon" (Subconscious Blockage)

- What thought, belief, or emotional pattern keeps coming up and holding you back?

- Common examples:
  ✓ "I'm not good enough."
  ✓ "I always fail."
  ✓ "Money is stressful."
  ✓ "People always leave me."

- Identify the **dominant negative thought** and the **emotion attached to it**.

Step 2: Engaging the Neurovascular Points to Interrupt the Emotional Pattern

231

The subconscious self is deeply connected to **specific points on the body** that regulate emotional responses.

✓ Place your fingertips gently on your **main frontal neurovascular points** (the center of your forehead).
✓ At the same time, use your other hand to **touch the neurovascular points just in front of your ears**.
✓ Focus on the limiting thought while **breathing deeply and holding these points**.
✓ This **interrupts the stress response** and **begins the emotional release process**.

Step 3: Using Emotional Freedom Technique (EFT) to Clear Resistance

- EFT (Tapping) uses specific meridian points to **dissolve emotional charge**.

- Tap lightly on the following sequence of points while stating the limiting belief:

  1. **Side of the hand (Karate chop point)**

  2. **Eyebrow point**

  3. **Side of the eye**

  4. **Under the eye**

  5. **Under the nose**

  6. **Chin**

  7. **Collarbone point**

  8. **Under the arm**

  9. **Top of the head**

- Repeat the process while **shifting the statement from negative to positive**:
  ✓ "Even though I feel [emotion], I deeply love and accept

myself."

✓ "I now release this belief and replace it with [new belief]."

By combining **neurovascular point activation and EFT**, the **Personal Demon Demolisher neutralizes emotional resistance**, allowing the subconscious self to **accept new, empowering patterns**.

Ho'oponopono: The Hawaiian Process for Emotional Clearing

Ho'oponopono is an ancient Hawaiian practice of **reconciliation, forgiveness, and emotional purification**. It is based on the understanding that **all external problems originate from internal subconscious patterns**.

By clearing these patterns, you restore harmony within yourself and in your external reality.

"The world you experience is a mirror of your subconscious self. If there is conflict, limitation, or struggle, it is a reflection of what exists within you."

Step 1: Identifying the Emotional Block

- What situation, belief, or relationship feels **heavy, stuck, or resistant**?

- Where in your body do you feel emotional tension?

Step 2: Repeating the Four Core Ho'oponopono Statements

Ho'oponopono consists of **four simple but powerful phrases** that energetically dissolve emotional blockages.

1. **"I love you."** → Sends healing energy to the situation.

2. **"I'm sorry."** → Acknowledges the subconscious pattern that needs clearing.

3. **"Please forgive me."** → Releases stored emotional resistance.

4. **"Thank you."** → Affirms completion and healing.

233

These statements **do not require knowing the exact root cause** of the issue. The subconscious self already knows **what needs to be released**, and this process **initiates the clearing automatically**.

Step 3: Feeling the Shift and Releasing Emotional Weight

- As you repeat the statements, **tune into any emotional changes**.

- If resistance comes up, **breathe deeply and continue the process**.

- Many people experience a **lightening of emotional weight, tingling sensations, or a deep sense of peace** after Ho'oponopono practice.

By performing Ho'oponopono regularly, you **clear subconscious emotional imprints**, making it easier to align with success, joy, and abundance.

The Next Step: Integrating Clearing Work into Daily Life
Now that we've explored two of the most **effective techniques for emotional clearing**, the next section will focus on:

✓ How to **combine these methods for maximum effect**.
✓ How to **recognize when deeper clearing is needed**.
✓ How to **prevent old patterns from returning**.

When clearing work becomes **a regular practice**, subconscious resistance disappears, and alignment with success happens **effortlessly**.

Key Takeaways from Section 6
💡 **Emotional clearing is essential before installing new subconscious beliefs.**
💡 **The Personal Demon Demolisher neutralizes emotional**

resistance and subconscious sabotage.

💡 Ho'oponopono dissolves emotional blocks at their root through forgiveness and reconciliation.

💡 Both methods work by clearing stored emotional patterns from the subconscious self.

💡 The next step is learning how to integrate these techniques into daily practice for lasting transformation.

Section 7 – Method 1: The Personal Demon Demolisher

Now that we understand the importance of clearing subconscious resistance, let's dive deeper into the **Personal Demon Demolisher**—a powerful technique for **eliminating emotional barriers, self-sabotage, and limiting beliefs** that block success.

The **Personal Demon Demolisher** works by:
✓ **Identifying and isolating the subconscious block.**
✓ **Interrupting the stress response tied to the belief.**
✓ **Dissolving the emotional charge using energy-based techniques.**
✓ **Replacing the limiting belief with a resourceful, empowered thought pattern.**

This method combines **neurovascular point activation and Emotional Freedom Technique (EFT, also known as Tapping)** to **release stored emotional resistance** and reprogram the subconscious self with new, aligned beliefs.

Identifying Your Personal Demon: The Hidden Emotional Block
A "personal demon" is **any subconscious belief that actively contradicts what you want to achieve**.

Common examples include:
✓ **"I'm not good enough."**

235

✓ "Success is too hard."
✓ "I always mess things up."
✓ "I'll never be financially free."
✓ "I don't deserve happiness."

These beliefs are often **ingrained from childhood experiences, social conditioning, or past failures** and operate **beneath conscious awareness**.

How to Identify Your Personal Demon:

1. Think about your **biggest goal**—something you truly desire.

2. Notice the **first negative thought, doubt, or resistance** that arises.

3. Pay attention to **how it feels in your body** (tightness, discomfort, anxiety).

4. Write down the **exact limiting belief or emotional reaction** that comes up.

This belief is **the subconscious barrier** that must be cleared before you can move forward.

Step 1: Engaging the Neurovascular Points to Interrupt the Emotional Pattern
When an emotional block is activated, the body **automatically enters a stress response**, which makes it harder to think clearly or take action.

To neutralize this response, we use **neurovascular activation**, which involves **lightly holding specific points on the head** to **shift the body from stress mode into relaxation mode**.

✓ Place your fingertips gently on your main frontal **neurovascular points** (the center of your forehead).
✓ With your other hand, touch the neurovascular points just in front of your ears.

✓ Focus on the limiting belief or emotional block while breathing deeply.

✓ Hold these points for at least **60–90 seconds**, or until you feel a **sense of release or relaxation**.

"The subconscious self cannot hold onto an emotional pattern once the body enters a state of deep relaxation."

This step **interrupts the subconscious feedback loop**, weakening the emotional charge behind the limiting belief.

Step 2: Using Emotional Freedom Technique (EFT) to Clear Resistance

EFT, or **Tapping**, is a powerful method that involves **gently tapping on specific meridian points** to release subconscious resistance and dissolve negative emotions.

The sequence follows these **nine key points**:

1. **Side of the hand (Karate Chop Point)** – Activates subconscious acceptance.

2. **Eyebrow point** – Releases stress and worry.

3. **Side of the eye** – Clears subconscious fears.

4. **Under the eye** – Neutralizes stored emotional trauma.

5. **Under the nose** – Releases subconscious self-judgment.

6. **Chin point** – Dissolves doubt and insecurity.

7. **Collarbone point** – Restores confidence and inner strength.

8. **Under the arm** – Clears resistance to change.

9. **Top of the head** – Reinforces new subconscious programming.

How to Use EFT for Clearing:

✓ **Begin by stating the limiting belief:**

- Example: *"Even though I feel like I'm not good enough, I deeply and completely accept myself."*
  ✓ **Tap through each of the nine points while repeating this statement.**
  ✓ **As the emotional charge weakens, introduce a new empowering belief:**

- Example: *"I now choose to believe in my worth and abilities."*
  ✓ **Repeat the process until the negative emotion is fully neutralized.**

"The subconscious self cannot hold onto limiting beliefs once the associated emotional charge has been dissolved."

EFT **disconnects emotional triggers from limiting beliefs**, allowing the subconscious self to **accept a new, empowered reality**.

Step 3: Replacing the Old Pattern with a Resourceful Thought-Form

Once the emotional charge is cleared, the subconscious self **must be given a new instruction** to replace the old limiting belief.

✓ **Step 1: Choose a new belief that aligns with success.**

- Example: *"I am worthy of success and abundance."*
  ✓ **Step 2: Engage in Multi-Sensory Thought-Form Creation (See Chapter 3).**

- Visualize yourself **living this belief** as if it is already true.

- Engage **sight, sound, touch, and emotion** to make it feel real.
  ✓ **Step 3: Reinforce the belief with strong positive emotions.**

- Feel **excitement, gratitude, and joy** while repeating the new belief.

"The subconscious self locks onto whatever is most emotionally intense. The stronger the feeling, the faster the belief takes root."

By consistently reinforcing the new belief **with strong emotions and sensory engagement**, the subconscious self **fully integrates it into reality**.

Using the Personal Demon Demolisher in Daily Life

To ensure lasting results, use the **Personal Demon Demolisher** regularly:

✔ **Before major events or challenges** – Clear emotional resistance before taking action.
✔ **Whenever self-doubt arises** – Interrupt negative patterns before they take hold.
✔ **Daily subconscious maintenance** – Prevent old patterns from resurfacing.

With consistent practice, limiting beliefs and subconscious resistance **dissolve completely**, making success effortless.

The Next Step: Ho'oponopono for Deeper Emotional Clearing

Now that we've explored the **Personal Demon Demolisher**, the next section will introduce:

✔ **The Hawaiian practice of Ho'oponopono for clearing subconscious resistance.**
✔ **How forgiveness and reconciliation dissolve deep emotional imprints.**
✔ **How to apply Ho'oponopono to relationships, abundance, and self-healing.**

By combining these two powerful techniques, subconscious transformation becomes **rapid, lasting, and effortless**.

Key Takeaways from Section 7
💡 **The Personal Demon Demolisher neutralizes emotional**

resistance at the subconscious level.

💡 Holding neurovascular points interrupts stress responses tied to limiting beliefs.

💡 EFT (Tapping) clears emotional blocks and rewires subconscious programming.

💡 Replacing old patterns with multi-sensory thought-forms ensures lasting transformation.

💡 The next step is using Ho'oponopono to dissolve emotional imprints at their deepest level.

Section 8 – Method 2: Ho'oponopono

Now that we have explored the **Personal Demon Demolisher** as a powerful tool for clearing subconscious resistance, let's introduce a second method: **Ho'oponopono**.

Ho'oponopono is an **ancient Hawaiian practice** of **reconciliation, forgiveness, and emotional purification**. It works by clearing subconscious emotional imprints that shape your reality—many of which you may not even be consciously aware of.

This technique is based on the understanding that **all external problems originate from internal subconscious patterns**. By clearing these patterns, you restore **harmony, alignment, and flow** within yourself and your external world.

The Philosophy Behind Ho'oponopono

Ho'oponopono is rooted in the idea that:

✓ Your reality is a reflection of your subconscious self.
✓ If you experience struggle, pain, or limitation, it is a signal that something in your subconscious needs clearing.
✓ By clearing the subconscious distortion, you resolve external challenges effortlessly.

Dr. Ihaleakala Hew Len, a modern practitioner of Ho'oponopono, demonstrated its power in a dramatic way. He worked at a **Hawaiian psychiatric hospital for the criminally insane** but instead of treating the patients directly, he applied Ho'oponopono by **clearing his own subconscious perceptions of them**.

✓ He repeatedly practiced Ho'oponopono using **four core statements**.
✓ Over time, patients who were previously considered untreatable **began to heal, improve, and eventually be released**.
✓ The hospital was eventually closed because there were **no more patients left to treat**.

This case illustrates how **clearing subconscious distortions within ourselves** has a profound **ripple effect** on the external world.

"Healing yourself heals the world, because everything you experience is an extension of your subconscious self."

The Four Core Statements of Ho'oponopono
At the heart of Ho'oponopono are **four simple but powerful phrases** that work together to dissolve emotional resistance and subconscious imprints.

1. **"I love you."** → Sends healing energy to the situation.

2. **"I'm sorry."** → Acknowledges the subconscious pattern that needs clearing.

3. **"Please forgive me."** → Releases stored emotional resistance.

4. **"Thank you."** → Affirms completion and healing.

When spoken with intention and feeling, these phrases **neutralize emotional blocks, release subconscious distortions, and realign your inner world with clarity and peace**.

How to Use Ho'oponopono for Emotional Clearing

This process does not require you to know the **exact cause** of the emotional resistance you are clearing. The subconscious self already **knows what needs to be released**, and Ho'oponopono initiates the clearing automatically.

Step 1: Identify the Emotional Block

- Bring to mind **any situation, person, or belief that feels heavy or resistant**.

- Notice where you **feel tension in your body** (chest, stomach, shoulders, etc.).

- Accept that **whatever is coming up is ready to be cleared**.

Step 2: Repeat the Four Ho'oponopono Statements

- Softly repeat:

    1. **"I love you."** (Sending love to the subconscious pattern.)

    2. **"I'm sorry."** (Acknowledging its presence.)

    3. **"Please forgive me."** (Allowing release and healing.)

    4. **"Thank you."** (Affirming that the clearing is complete.)

- Say these phrases **slowly and with feeling** until you **feel a shift in your emotional state**.

- If resistance arises, **breathe through it and continue**.

Expanding Ho'oponopono for Deeper Healing

While the **four core phrases** work on their own, advanced Ho'oponopono practitioners also use **Morrnah Simeona's expanded version.**

This prayer calls upon the **Transcendent Self** to clear subconscious emotional imprints **from all past generations, timelines, and dimensions**.

The Expanded Ho'oponopono Prayer:

"Divine Creator, Father, Mother, Son as One...
If I, my family, relatives, and ancestors have offended you, your family, relatives, and ancestors in thoughts, words, deeds, and actions, from the beginning of our creation to the present, we ask your forgiveness.
Let this cleanse, purify, release, and cut all the negative memories, blocks, energies, and vibrations, and transmute them into pure light.
And it is done."

This version is **especially effective for clearing deep generational patterns**, subconscious trauma, and emotional imprints from past experiences.

How Ho'oponopono Works in Relationships, Abundance, and Health

Ho'oponopono can be applied to **any area of life** where resistance, struggle, or emotional weight exists.

✓ **For Relationships:**

- If you are experiencing conflict, instead of focusing on **what the other person did wrong**, repeat the Ho'oponopono phrases internally.

- As you clear subconscious distortions, you **change the dynamic energetically**, and the external relationship shifts accordingly.

✓ **For Abundance:**

- If financial struggle persists, practice Ho'oponopono **on your beliefs about money**.

- Example: **"I love you, I'm sorry, please forgive me, thank you,"** directed toward any discomfort around wealth.

✓ **For Health and Healing:**

- If physical symptoms arise, instead of fighting them, apply Ho'oponopono to **your body, cells, and subconscious health beliefs**.

- This has been shown to accelerate **healing and emotional well-being**.

"Ho'oponopono does not fix the external world—it clears the subconscious distortions that created the external world in the first place."

The Next Step: Integrating Both Clearing Methods for Maximum Transformation

Now that we've explored **Ho'oponopono**, the next section will introduce:

✓ How to **combine Ho'oponopono with the Personal Demon Demolisher** for deeper subconscious clearing.
✓ How to **know when more clearing is needed** before moving forward.
✓ How to **prevent old patterns from resurfacing**.

By making **clearing work a regular practice**, subconscious blocks dissolve, and success becomes **a natural state of being**.

Key Takeaways from Section 8
💡 **Ho'oponopono clears subconscious distortions that shape external reality.**
💡 **The four core phrases dissolve emotional resistance and subconscious blocks.**
💡 **Healing yourself internally leads to transformation in the**

external world.

💡 Expanded Ho'oponopono can clear deep generational and karmic patterns.

💡 The next step is learning how to integrate both clearing methods for permanent subconscious reprogramming.

Section 9 – Putting It All Together: The Path to Emotional Freedom

Now that we have explored two of the most **powerful subconscious clearing techniques**, the next step is understanding **how to integrate them into daily life** for lasting transformation.

Emotional clearing is not a **one-time fix**—it is an ongoing process of **identifying, clearing, and replacing** subconscious patterns as they arise.

By consistently practicing the **Personal Demon Demolisher** and **Ho'oponopono**, you create a subconscious environment that is **free of resistance, open to success, and aligned with your highest potential**.

The Role of Clearing Work in the MSM® System

Clearing subconscious resistance is a **critical step** in the **Master the Science of Miracles® (MSM®) system**. Without clearing:

✔ **Negative thought-forms continue to cycle, blocking manifestation.**
✔ **The subconscious self resists change, reinforcing old patterns.**
✔ **Emotional misalignment prevents multi-sensory thought-forms from taking root.**

Once subconscious resistance is cleared:

✔ **Your subconscious self fully supports your goals.**
✔ **Multi-sensory thought-forms (See Chapter 3) become highly**

effective.
✓ **Manifestation accelerates effortlessly, without struggle.**

"The more you clear subconscious resistance, the less effort is required to create your desired reality."

By making emotional clearing a **regular practice**, success becomes **inevitable**.

Combining Both Methods for Maximum Effectiveness
Both **The Personal Demon Demolisher** and **Ho'oponopono** are effective on their own, but **using them together creates a complete subconscious clearing system.**

How to Use Both Methods in Sequence:

1. **Use the Personal Demon Demolisher to Clear Immediate Resistance**

   o When a negative thought or emotional trigger arises, **apply neurovascular activation and EFT tapping** to neutralize it.

   o This method is **best for specific, recurring subconscious blocks** (e.g., "I'm not good enough," "I always fail," "Money is stressful").

2. **Use Ho'oponopono to Dissolve Deeper Emotional Imprints**

   o If you notice patterns of struggle in relationships, finances, or health, use **Ho'oponopono to clear subconscious distortions at the root level**.

   o This method is **best for clearing unknown or generational subconscious patterns** (e.g., deep-seated fears, family conditioning, karmic imprints).

By alternating these two techniques based on **the nature of the subconscious resistance**, you ensure that **all levels of emotional blockages are addressed.**

How to Recognize When More Clearing Is Needed
Even after doing clearing work, **subconscious patterns can sometimes resurface**. This is normal, as layers of programming are released over time.

Signs that more clearing is needed:
✓ You experience **strong emotional reactions** to challenges.
✓ You feel **stuck, overwhelmed, or resistant** to taking action.
✓ You notice **repeating patterns** in relationships, finances, or health.
✓ Your **affirmations or visualizations feel forced or unconvincing**.

Whenever these signs appear, it is a **signal that deeper subconscious clearing is required**.

"Every time resistance arises, it is an opportunity for deeper subconscious transformation."

Instead of viewing resistance as **a setback**, see it as **an invitation to clear the next layer of subconscious programming**.

Preventing Old Patterns from Returning
Once an emotional block is cleared, the subconscious self **may attempt to revert to familiar patterns**. To prevent this:

✓ **Immediately reinforce the new belief with Multi-Sensory Thought-Forms (See Chapter 3).**
✓ **Use daily clearing rituals** to keep subconscious resistance low.
✓ **Monitor your language (See Section 4) to ensure you are programming the subconscious with success-focused statements.**
✓ **Practice emotional awareness**—catch negative thought loops early before they strengthen.

By remaining conscious of **subconscious patterns as they arise**, you ensure that **old beliefs never regain control**.

Moving Forward with Clarity and Confidence

Now that you have a **complete system for clearing subconscious resistance**, the final step is making **these practices a part of your daily routine**.

When emotional clearing becomes **second nature**, you experience:

✓ **Freedom from past limitations.**
✓ **Deep alignment between your subconscious and conscious desires.**
✓ **A natural, effortless connection to success, abundance, and joy.**

"When resistance is cleared, miracles become normal."

With these techniques, you **remove the barriers that once held you back** and step fully into your **highest potential**.

Final Thoughts on Chapter 7

💡 **Your subconscious self is always listening—reprogram it to say YES to what you truly desire.**

💡 **Negative emotions are not obstacles—they are signals guiding you toward healing.**

💡 **Clearing emotional resistance makes manifestation effortless.**

💡 **Using both The Personal Demon Demolisher and Ho'oponopono creates deep subconscious transformation.**

💡 **Making emotional clearing a daily practice ensures permanent alignment with success.**

Chapter 8: The Transcendent Self

Section 1 – Understanding the Transcendent Self

The *Master the Science of Miracles®* system is built upon a foundational understanding of the three aspects of the self: the conscious self, the subconscious self, and the Transcendent Self. Of these three, the **Transcendent Self** is the most exalted, least understood, and most often overlooked. It is not bound by time, space, or sensory perception. It is **the eternal, spiritual essence within you**, the part of you that was never born and will never die.

While the subconscious self can be trained and the conscious self developed, the Transcendent Self is not something to be "improved." It is already perfect. What can be developed, however, is your **awareness of and relationship with it**.

To speak of the Transcendent Self is to necessarily enter territory that sounds spiritual or religious. But *Master the Science of Miracles®* is **not a religion**. It doesn't require you to adopt any particular belief system or reject your current one. It is a system that works **whether you call the Transcendent Self your Higher Self, the divine spark, the Spirit within, or simply the unknowable aspect of consciousness.**

Throughout history, humanity has used different names for this deepest part of the self, but the experience it points to is **universal**. Unfortunately, people often confuse the **lamp** with the **light**—they cling to the forms and rituals of religion, forgetting that the purpose of the form is to deliver the formless: **the light of truth, love, and spiritual awareness**.

Master the Science of Miracles® honors all spiritual traditions—and transcends them. It does not ask you to trade your lamp for a new one. It simply helps you focus on the **light** shining from within it. The **Transcendent Self is that light**—the source of guidance, inspiration, intuition, healing, and revelation.

In this chapter, we will explore the nature of the Transcendent Self, how it relates to the conscious and subconscious selves, and how you can begin to build a **clear, intentional relationship** with this most sacred dimension of who you are.

When you do, you will discover what the mystics and masters of every tradition have taught:

"Everything in the universe is within you. Ask all from yourself." – Rumi

Let us begin.

Section 2 – The Three Aspects of the Self

To understand the Transcendent Self, it helps to first review how it fits within the full structure of the human being as presented in MSM. There are **three distinct aspects of the self** that together form the whole person:

1. **The Conscious Self**

2. **The Subconscious Self**

3. **The Transcendent Self**

Each of these has its own characteristics, functions, and ways of interacting with reality. While modern psychology recognizes only the conscious and subconscious (or unconscious) mind, MSM goes further by acknowledging the third and highest aspect—the Transcendent Self.

---

1. The Conscious Self

This is the aspect most people identify with. It is the "you" who thinks, analyzes, evaluates, plans, and speaks. It is the seat of logic, reason, and decision-making. In psychological terms, it corresponds to Freud's **ego** or Jung's **conscious mind**.

While the conscious self is essential for navigating day-to-day life, it operates in **linear time** and has limited access to the vast database of stored experiences and emotions held in the subconscious.

2. The Subconscious Self

The subconscious self is like a powerful computer running behind the scenes. It **stores every experience** you've ever had, along with all the emotions, sensations, and beliefs formed throughout your life.

It regulates all **autonomic bodily functions** and influences your behaviors, habits, emotional responses, and even your perception of what is possible.

While the conscious self can make choices, it is the **subconscious self that carries them out**, often without question—unless old programming or emotional blocks are standing in the way.

3. The Transcendent Self

The Transcendent Self stands apart from the other two. It does not arise from experience, biology, or memory. It is not a product of learning or evolution. Instead, it is **eternal, divine, and nonlocal**— meaning it exists outside the bounds of time and space.

It does not reside in a location within the body, nor can it be seen, touched, or measured. In quantum terms, it behaves like a **nonlocal entity**—not present in any one place, yet **able to influence all places at once**.

It is your **deepest reality**, your direct connection to the Source of all that is. And while you may not perceive it through your five senses, you can experience it through its **effects**—intuition, revelation, healing, grace, and spiritual insight.

The conscious self analyzes.
The subconscious self remembers and reacts.
The Transcendent Self **knows**.

The relationship among these three aspects of self is central to the entire MSM system. The conscious self **forms the desire**, the subconscious self **energizes and transmits it**, and the Transcendent Self **brings it into form**—or offers redirection toward something better.

In the next section, we'll explore how various spiritual traditions and psychological frameworks have attempted to describe this highest part of the self—and why none of them can fully capture it.

Section 3 – Attempts to Describe the Transcendent Self

The Transcendent Self, by its very nature, defies precise description. It is a reality that exists beyond the reach of the five senses, beyond thought, and even beyond imagination. And yet, throughout history, humanity has sought to describe it in metaphors, myths, and mystical language—attempts that are always partial, yet often deeply meaningful.

Many spiritual traditions refer to this aspect of the self as the **Higher Self**, the **Atman**, the **Oversoul**, the **Divine Spark**, or the **Christ within**. In MSM, we use the term **Transcendent Self** to avoid religious overtones and to point clearly to its non-material, universal nature.

Shamanic Descriptions

In Polynesian and Hawaiian shamanism, the Transcendent Self was described as the *Utterly Trustworthy Parental Spirit*. It was revered as **the highest, most refined part of a person**—wise, compassionate, infinitely patient, and always ready to help.

These traditions taught that this spirit could not be commanded or manipulated. It could only be approached with **reverence, humility,**

and clarity. Communication with it required the cooperation of the subconscious self, which served as the messenger between the conscious and Transcendent Selves.

This view beautifully mirrors the MSM understanding: that the conscious self must work through the subconscious self to **reach the Transcendent Self**, and that emotional clarity and purity of intent are essential for that connection.

A More Elegant Description

While the shamanic image of a benevolent, parental spirit is helpful, one of the most elegant and elevated descriptions of the Transcendent Self comes from 'Abdu'l-Bahá, the son of Bahá'u'lláh, founder of the Bahá'í Faith. He speaks of the third reality in man as the **spiritual reality**, and what he says about it aligns perfectly with the core of MSM.

He explains that this aspect of the self is:

- **Indestructible**, belonging to the world of the divine and supernatural.

- **Eternal**, not subject to birth or death.

- **The source of illumination**, allowing us to perceive spiritual realities.

- **The channel for revelation**, enabling glimpses of the past and the future.

- **Liberating**, delivering the human being from the limitations of the material world.

- **Capable of achieving the infinitude of the Creator**, through its divine capacity.

This is not merely poetic language—it is a profound **metaphysical insight**. The Transcendent Self is that which **connects you directly to**

253

the Infinite. It is not separate from the Source; it is a **ray of that same sun**, shining into your soul.

You cannot see it, but you can feel its warmth.
You cannot touch it, but you can be transformed by its light.

The more you come to recognize its presence, the more it becomes a **reliable partner in your inner and outer life**. In the MSM system, this relationship becomes not only possible—but central.

In the next section, we will explore how contact with the Transcendent Self actually occurs—and why the subconscious self is the indispensable link between you and this highest part of yourself.

Section 4 – Interaction with the Transcendent Self

One of the most important insights offered by the Master the Science of Miracles® system is that **the conscious self cannot interact directly with the Transcendent Self**.

This can be a surprising idea—especially for those who have long sought to connect with the divine through willpower, focused thought, or conscious intention alone. But the structure of the self, as understood in MSM, makes it clear: **the Transcendent Self does not speak the language of the conscious mind**.

Why the Conscious Self Cannot Make Direct Contact

The conscious self operates through **logic, linear time, and verbal language**. It is bound by the rules of physical space and causality. The Transcendent Self, by contrast, is **nonverbal, nonlocal, nonlinear, and nonphysical**. It cannot be accessed through analysis or effort of will—no matter how noble the intention.

It is not because the Transcendent Self is withholding or distant. Quite the opposite—it is **always ready to assist**. But the conscious self is simply **not equipped to receive its impressions directly**.

Trying to connect to the Transcendent Self through intellect is like trying to hear a melody by looking at the sheet music—it may point you in the right direction, but it **isn't the experience itself.**

The Role of the Subconscious Self as Intermediary
In MSM, the **subconscious self serves as the only viable channel** between the conscious self and the Transcendent Self.

It functions as a **messenger and translator**—capable of understanding the emotional language of the conscious self and the symbolic, energetic communication of the Transcendent Self.

✓ When you create a vivid, emotionally-charged thought-form, it is the subconscious self that **packages it** and conveys it upward to the Transcendent Self.
✓ When the Transcendent Self sends insight, intuition, or inspiration, it is the subconscious self that **decodes and delivers** the message back to the conscious mind—often in the form of dreams, emotional impressions, sudden clarity, or synchronicities.

This is why **clearing subconscious blocks (Chapter 7) and developing a cooperative relationship with the subconscious self (Chapters 4 and 5)** are critical.

If the subconscious is confused, cluttered, or emotionally overwhelmed, **messages to and from the Transcendent Self are distorted or blocked altogether**.

The Transcendent Self is always transmitting.
The question is: *Is your subconscious self tuned in to receive it?*

MSM as a Bridge to the Transcendent
The purpose of the *Master the Science of Miracles®* system is not just to help you manifest external outcomes. It is to help you **realign the three aspects of your being**, so they operate in **unified harmony**.

When the conscious self, subconscious self, and Transcendent Self are aligned:

✓ Desire flows clearly upward.

✓ Insight flows clearly downward.

✓ The bridge between the human and the divine is fully open.

In the next section, we'll explore **how you can recognize the presence of the Transcendent Self—not through seeing or hearing it directly, but by perceiving its radiant effects in your life.**

Section 5 – Knowing the Transcendent Self Through Its Attributes

Because the Transcendent Self exists beyond physical perception, it cannot be known directly through the five senses. But just as you know the sun exists—not because you can look at it directly, but because you feel its warmth and see by its light—you come to know the Transcendent Self **by the qualities it expresses through your life.**

This is one of the key insights of MSM:

You don't know the Transcendent Self by its form—you know it by its effects.

The more you become aware of these effects, the more tangible and real the presence of the Transcendent Self becomes in your day-to-day experience.

The Attributes of the Transcendent Self

You've already felt the presence of your Transcendent Self—whether or not you realized it at the time.

It reveals itself in fleeting moments when the noise of the mind grows quiet, and a deeper presence arises—still, loving, wise, and whole. Some of the clearest expressions of the Transcendent Self include:

- **Unconditional love** that feels vast and limitless.

- **Deep compassion** for others, even strangers.

- **Profound forgiveness**, especially when it seems undeserved.

- **Sudden inspiration or inner knowing** that feels like it came from nowhere.

- **Awe and reverence** in the presence of beauty, truth, or the sacred.

These aren't just elevated emotions. They are **signals of contact** with something greater than the individual self. The Transcendent Self is making itself known.

Everyday Examples of Divine Attributes
You may have already had moments like these:

✓ The overwhelming tenderness of holding a newborn child.
✓ The sudden clarity that tells you what to do when logic fails.
✓ The comfort that arrives in the middle of grief, unbidden but real.
✓ The sense of being wrapped in love during meditation or prayer.
✓ The beauty of a night sky that stirs something ancient in your soul.

These moments are not emotional accidents.
They are **echoes of the Transcendent Self**, breaking through.

When you experience a wave of compassion for a person you would normally resent...
When you feel deeply seen and accepted despite your flaws...
When you forgive someone and feel the burden lift...

...you are not just having a better day—you are **tasting divine attributes** flowing through your own being.

The Transcendent Self Knows and Loves You Completely
Perhaps the most reassuring truth MSM offers is this:

Your Transcendent Self knows everything about you and cherishes you anyway.

It knows your fears, failures, doubts, and regrets—and none of it diminishes its love for you. In fact, it is **always ready to help** the moment you are willing to ask and receive.

If you've ever been on the receiving end of a grandmother's love—unconditional, tender, fierce in its protection—you've had a small glimpse of what the Transcendent Self feels toward you.

Only it's **stronger than that**.
Purer than that.
And **eternal**.

In the next section, we'll explore how this highest part of you communicates—not with words, but with **feeling, imagery, and impression**—and why the subconscious self is uniquely suited to interpret its messages.

Section 6 – The Language of the Transcendent Self

The Transcendent Self does not speak in words. It doesn't use language the way the conscious self does, nor does it communicate in logical thoughts or verbal commands. Instead, its messages are conveyed through a much subtler medium: **feeling, imagery, sensation, intuition, and energy**.

This creates a challenge for the conscious self, which is conditioned to rely on **rational thought and verbal dialogue** to make sense of the world. Fortunately, there is a part of you that understands the language of the Transcendent Self fluently: **your subconscious self**.

Why the Subconscious Self is the Translator

The subconscious self is intimately familiar with **nonverbal forms of communication**. It processes dreams, symbols, emotions, memories, sensations, and impressions with ease. It doesn't rely on speech. It doesn't analyze or debate. It receives and responds.

This makes the subconscious self the **ideal bridge** between the conscious and Transcendent Selves. When the Transcendent Self reaches out with a message, it is the subconscious self that:
✓ Receives the impulse.
✓ Interprets the energy.
✓ Translates it into symbols, sensations, or intuitive flashes.
✓ Passes the decoded message up to the conscious self—often as a "gut feeling," a dream, a visual image, or a sudden knowing.

This is why developing sensitivity to your emotional and intuitive landscape is essential.
It is **your subconscious self's way of speaking on behalf of the Transcendent.**

What the Transcendent Self Sends and Receives

When you communicate with the Transcendent Self, you aren't sending it sentences. You're sending it **a kind of energetic package—** what MSM refers to as a **multi-sensory thought-form** (covered in detail in Chapter 3).

✓ The conscious self conceives the desire.
✓ The subconscious self gives it emotional energy and imagery.
✓ The Transcendent Self receives the final form **not as a worded request, but as a living, felt experience**.

Likewise, when guidance, inspiration, or healing flows back from the Transcendent Self:
✓ It arrives not as a voice in your head, but as a **shift in perception**,
✓ a moment of **clarity**,
✓ a flood of **peace**,
✓ or a symbol in a dream that stirs something deep and unmistakable.

The Misstep of Expecting Words

Many spiritual seekers grow frustrated when they don't hear "answers" in response to their prayers or meditations. They expect God or Spirit to reply the same way a friend would in conversation. But the Transcendent Self is **not verbal**. It speaks in the language of **essence**—not form.

You won't always hear it.
You'll feel it.
And once you become attuned to that mode of communication, you'll recognize that it has **been speaking to you all along**.

In the next section, we'll revisit the concept of the multi-sensory thought-form and explore how this powerful tool becomes the **primary method of communication** between you and your Transcendent Self.

Section 7 – Creating Multi-Sensory Thought-Forms to Communicate with the Transcendent Self

In the MSM system, your clearest, most effective communication with the Transcendent Self happens through a specific vehicle: the **multi-sensory thought-form**. This is not a wish, a hope, or a vague intention. It is a **fully formed energetic structure**, crafted by the conscious self, energized by the subconscious self, and delivered through the heart to the Transcendent Self.

You were introduced to this process in Chapter 3. Here, we revisit it—not to repeat the steps, but to emphasize its deeper purpose: **to speak the language of the divine.**

What Is a Multi-Sensory Thought-Form?

A multi-sensory thought-form is a **vivid, detailed mental image** of the life you desire, constructed in your imagination as if it were

already happening. But it is more than just a picture—it is rich with emotion, color, sound, movement, and physical sensation.

This is not visualization in the shallow sense of "daydreaming about what you want." It is **an embodied inner experience**, designed to replicate the emotional, sensory, and energetic qualities of the outcome you wish to manifest.

When done properly, the subconscious self accepts it as **present reality**, and the Transcendent Self responds by orchestrating the outer conditions necessary to align your life with that inner experience.

How to Construct a Multi-Sensory Thought-Form
To communicate effectively with the Transcendent Self, the thought-form must feel **real, joyful, and emotionally charged**. Ask yourself:

- **What will I see when my goal is fully realized?**
  (Who's around me? What does the environment look like?)

- **What sounds will fill the space?**
  (Voices? Applause? Laughter? Silence?)

- **What physical sensations will I feel?**
  (Warmth? Comfort? The texture of what you touch?)

- **What will I smell or taste?**
  (Fresh air? A celebratory meal? Flowers?)

- **What emotions will be flooding my heart in that moment?**
  (Gratitude? Joy? Relief? Love?)

This thought-form becomes a kind of **living hologram**—an energetic blueprint. And when it is **infused with high-vibration emotions** like gratitude, awe, and love, it becomes **a spiritual offering**, presented through the subconscious to the Transcendent Self.

The Role of Emotion and Energy

It is not enough to simply think about what you want. The subconscious self is **not moved by neutral images**—it is activated by **feeling**. And the Transcendent Self is **energized by elevated states of consciousness**.

That's why every multi-sensory thought-form must be **charged with an emotional peak state**—a moment of real, felt connection to the experience. (See Chapters 3 and 7 for anchoring techniques and energy amplification.)

The more joy, wonder, and gratitude you can feel in the imagined experience,
the more clearly your subconscious self delivers it,
and the more powerfully your Transcendent Self responds.

Thought-Form as Sacred Language

You can think of the multi-sensory thought-form as **your soul's prayer in its native language**—a prayer without words, filled instead with vision, feeling, beauty, and light.

Unlike verbal affirmations, which may be contradicted by doubt or disbelief, the multi-sensory thought-form **bypasses the filters of the rational mind** and speaks directly to the divine within you.

In the next section, we'll explore how this "prayer form" is carried to the Transcendent Self through the heart—an organ far more mysterious and powerful than most people realize.

Section 8 – The Heart as the Portal to the Transcendent Self

In the MSM system, the **heart** is not just a physical organ—it is a **sacred portal**, a transformational center that serves as the bridge between the physical world of form and the spiritual world of essence.

It is through the heart that the **multi-sensory thought-form is transmitted to the Transcendent Self**.

When a student of MSM constructs a thought-form with care, infuses it with emotional power, and then directs it through the heart, something extraordinary occurs: the desire is **lifted out of the personal realm and offered into the universal**.

The Heart as a Step-Down and Step-Up Transformer

Just as a transformer regulates electrical current to make it usable at different voltages, the heart plays **two key energetic roles** in the communication between the human and the divine:

1. **Step-Down Transformer**

    o   It receives the subtle, high-frequency impulses from the Transcendent Self and steps them down into forms that the subconscious can register—impressions, feelings, symbols, and intuitive nudges.

    o   Without this translation, divine guidance would bypass your awareness altogether.

2. **Step-Up Transformer**

    o   When a vivid, emotionally-charged thought-form is generated by the conscious self and energized by the subconscious, the heart steps it up into **a high-frequency signal** suitable for transmission to the Transcendent Self.

    o   This is the moment the "prayer form" is released.

The **heart is not just metaphorically important—it is the metaphysical engine** that makes communion between human and divine possible.

Scientific and Mystical Perspectives

Modern research supports what mystics have long understood: the heart is more than a pump. It has its **own intelligence**, with a complex nervous system and energy field that **radiates far beyond the body**.

From a scientific standpoint:

- The heart has been shown to **emit an electromagnetic field** up to 5,000 times more powerful than that of the brain.

- It responds to **emotional states before the brain does**, suggesting it has its own awareness.

- Papillae on the surface of the heart contain nerve endings that **respond to subtle vibrations**, possibly spiritual in origin.

From a mystical standpoint:

- The heart has always been considered the **seat of the soul**, the home of divine love, and the **gateway to spiritual realms**.

- In countless traditions, **it is the place where heaven meets earth**, and where the finite touches the infinite.

How to Use the Heart as a Portal

When you've created your multi-sensory thought-form and charged it with high-vibration emotion, the final step is simple, yet sacred:

1. **Bring your awareness to the center of your chest.**

   o Imagine your heart glowing with warmth and light.

2. **Feel your thought-form gathering in your heart space.**

   o See it shimmering there—whole, beautiful, complete.

3. **Feel the stream of energy rise within you.**

   o This energy, developed and concentrated through your focused attention and emotional intensity, is what MSM refers to as **the energy of miracles**.

4. **On an exhale, release the thought-form upward through your heart.**

   o   Not by force, but with surrender.

   o   Not with strain, but with trust.

5. **Affirm silently or aloud:**

   o   *"I now offer this thought-form to my Transcendent Self, on a stream of love, joy, and gratitude."*

And then... let it go.

Receiving in Return

Once released, your role is not to obsess or analyze. It is to **remain open, grateful, and alert**. The Transcendent Self may respond immediately—or in time—but its reply will always be perfectly timed, and often more beautiful than what you imagined.

In the next section, we'll explore what it looks like to live with **active awareness of the Transcendent Self**—how to recognize its guidance, honor its presence, and integrate its influence into your everyday life.

Final Thoughts: The Transcendent Self in Daily Life

The ultimate goal of *Master the Science of Miracles*® is not just the creation of desired outcomes—it is the **reunion of your full self**. When the conscious self, subconscious self, and Transcendent Self are aligned, life takes on a quality of flow, presence, and meaning that transcends effort and control.

This chapter has explored the nature of your Transcendent Self: the eternal, indestructible core of your being that exists beyond time and space. But it's important to remember—this highest aspect of you is not reserved for mystical experiences or spiritual emergencies.

The Transcendent Self is meant to be a **daily companion**, a **steady presence**, and a **trusted guide**.

Recognizing the Presence of the Transcendent Self

The Transcendent Self doesn't announce itself with thunderclaps or visions (though it might). More often, it speaks in **subtle impressions and moments of knowing**. You may sense it:

- In the stillness that settles just before you fall asleep.

- In the sudden warmth of compassion for a stranger.

- In the inner voice that lovingly nudges you to call someone, change direction, or forgive.

- In the invisible hand that seems to rearrange your circumstances for the better.

These are not coincidences. They are **expressions of the divine within you**—the gentle signals of your Transcendent Self reminding you that you are never alone, never forgotten, never disconnected.

Making the Relationship Practical

In MSM, the relationship with the Transcendent Self is not theoretical—it's living and practical. Like any relationship, it grows stronger with attention and care. You deepen it by:

- **Creating and releasing multi-sensory thought-forms** regularly.

- **Starting each day with intention**—not just what you want to do, but *who you want to be aligned with*.

- **Listening for guidance** in your body, emotions, and intuition—not just your thoughts.

- **Offering gratitude often**—not only when things go well, but even before they do.

266

Small daily gestures—pausing in beauty, breathing deeply while holding a thought-form in your heart, honoring a feeling of inner peace—these are the sacred rituals that keep you connected.

A Life Guided from Within

Over time, as your awareness grows, you'll begin to recognize just how **active and reliable** the Transcendent Self truly is.

You'll feel less pressure to figure everything out with your mind.
You'll notice more ease in decisions, more flow in your efforts, more grace in your setbacks.
You'll learn to **trust what arises within you**, knowing that it comes from a part of you that sees what your eyes cannot.

And that's when the miracles become regular.
Not because the laws of the universe changed—
but because *you did*.

This is the gift of the Transcendent Self: a source of unconditional love, divine wisdom, and infinite support that is never far, always here, and already yours.

Key Takeaways from Chapter 8

💡 The Transcendent Self is your highest, eternal reality—beyond space, time, and form.

💡 It cannot be approached through logic, but it speaks through feeling, imagery, and energy.

💡 The subconscious self is the essential bridge for communication between the conscious and Transcendent Selves.

💡 Multi-sensory thought-forms, transmitted through the heart, are the clearest way to send intentions to the Transcendent Self.

💡 Awareness of the Transcendent Self turns ordinary moments into sacred ones—and life into a dialogue with the divine.

Chapter 9: Putting It All Together

Your Path to Miracles

Throughout this book, you've discovered that the life you live is not merely shaped by circumstances, fate, or random chance. It is shaped—moment by moment—by the **alignment and interaction of three distinct aspects of your being**: the conscious self, the subconscious self, and the Transcendent Self.

The *Master the Science of Miracles®* system is a step-by-step method for bringing these three selves into **clear communication and functional harmony** so that your desires are no longer just wishes—they become **living blueprints**, carried through the subconscious self and delivered to the Transcendent Self to be fulfilled in the world of form.

This chapter is your guide to **putting it all together**. What follows is a detailed, repeatable, and sacred process that enables you to co-create miracles in your life by forming and transmitting a **thought-form prayer**.

Step 1 – Establish a Clear Desire

Begin with clarity. You must know what you want to experience—not just as a vague wish, but as a **definite outcome**. This doesn't mean obsessing over every detail, but it does mean selecting a desire that is **emotionally compelling and meaningful to you**.

Ask yourself:

- What do I want to experience as if it were already true?

- How will my life feel when this is part of my reality?

Choose one desire for each thought-form prayer. The subconscious self works best when the signal is clear and undiluted.

Step 2 – Create a Word Picture of Your Desired Reality
Using your imagination, construct a **word picture** of what your life will look like when this desire is fully realized. Write it down or speak it aloud.

Focus on:

- Who is with you?

- What are you doing?

- What's happening around you?

- What can you see, hear, and feel?

Use vivid language, sensory details, and present-tense phrasing. Let it feel real, current, and alive.

Step 3 – Recall and Anchor a Peak Emotional State
To charge the word picture with energy, you must first generate an **elevated emotional state**. Recall a memory of a moment when you felt deep love, awe, gratitude, joy, or reverence.

Examples include:

- Holding your newborn child

- Gazing at a vast night sky

- Standing before a waterfall

- Experiencing unconditional love

Relive this memory fully. As you do, **anchor the emotional state** by pressing two fingers to your heart center or placing your hands over your chest. Breathe slowly. Let the emotion expand through your entire body.

Step 4 – Create a Multi-Sensory Thought-Form

Now, combine the word picture and the peak state. Using your inner senses, **step into the scene you described**.

✓ See what you would see
✓ Hear what you would hear
✓ Feel textures, sensations, and emotional tones
✓ Taste, smell, and move within this desired reality

Experience it as though it were **happening now**. Allow yourself to smile, laugh, cry, or feel awe. Let your subconscious self be fully engaged.

You are now creating the **prayer form**—a fully energized, emotionally-charged, multi-sensory signal encoded with your desired reality.

Step 5 – Direct the Thought-Form to the Heart Portal

Bring the entire experience—the images, the emotions, the sensory data—into your heart center. Imagine it gathering there like a radiant sphere of light, pulsing with life and joy.

As you feel the energy build, affirm silently or aloud:

"I now offer this thought-form to my Transcendent Self, on a stream of love, joy, and gratitude."

Breathe into your heart and, on the exhale, **release the prayer form upward**—not by force, but with trust.

You have now transmitted the thought-form prayer.

Step 6 – Surrender, Listen, and Follow
After releasing the prayer form, your job is not to chase or force results. Your job is to:

- **Stay open and alert**
- **Watch for signs, insights, and synchronicities**
- **Act on intuitive nudges**
- **Clear resistance as it arises (see Chapter 7)**
- **Repeat the process as needed, always with joy and reverence**

The Transcendent Self responds not to desperation or manipulation, but to **clarity, gratitude, and trust**.

Final Encouragement: Make This Your Way of Life
This is not a trick or technique. It's a way of **living in harmony with who you truly are**. The more you walk this path, the more effortless miracles become—not because life becomes easy, but because **you become aligned** with your deepest source of power, wisdom, and love.

You are no longer a beggar hoping for scraps of good fortune.
You are a **co-creator**, a vessel of light,
a living expression of the infinite made manifest in human form.

Use this system with love. Use it with awe. Use it with faith.

The Transcendent Self is listening.

Key Takeaways from Chapter 9
💡 The conscious self imagines, the subconscious self energizes, and the Transcendent Self manifests.
💡 Multi-sensory thought-forms are the language of effective prayer.

💡 The heart is the portal—always open, always sacred.

💡 Elevated emotion is the power source that illuminates the prayer form.

💡 Surrender is not weakness—it is cooperation with divine intelligence.

💡 The miracle you seek is seeking you.

Epilogue

The Light Was Always Yours

As you reach the final page of this book, I want to offer you something more than a conclusion. I want to offer you a blessing.

Not the kind spoken over you from above, but the kind **drawn out of you from within**—because the truth is, **you were never separate from the Source you've been seeking**. The light, the love, the wisdom, the power... it has always been there, quietly waiting behind the noise, the doubt, and the forgetting.

This system—*Master the Science of Miracles*®—is not something I invented. It's something I discovered, through decades of study, practice, breakdowns, and breakthroughs. Like you, I was searching. Like you, I wanted more than achievement, more than success. I wanted to live from a place of joy. Of meaning. Of truth.

And I learned—sometimes the hard way—that **miracles don't come from striving harder. They come from aligning deeper.** They come from reconnecting the three sacred parts of your being, and then letting the Transcendent Self lead.

Now that you know how to create and deliver a thought-form prayer, I invite you to begin. Not perfectly. Not forcefully. But honestly. With reverence. With hope.

You don't have to master the system before using it. You simply have to begin.

Make space for the Transcendent Self to work in your life. Make time to listen. Let joy become your fuel, not your reward. Let your prayers be offerings, not bargains.

And when you feel resistance, when doubt creeps in, or life gets messy—remember, you're not alone. This path is not a solo journey. **It's a shared awakening.**

I walk it with you.

And when you're ready to go further—when you want support, insight, or partnership—I'll be here, offering the same light that was once offered to me.

But for now, I leave you with this:

You are the miracle.
The light you seek is already burning in you.
Ask all from yourself—and give all to the world.

Until we meet again,
Walk with love. Walk with power. Walk with the Transcendent Self beside you.

About the Author

Ron Matthews is a true renaissance man—a rare soul who has walked with equal mastery through the realms of science and spirit.

With over 35 years as an engineer and physicist, Ron has contributed to some of the world's most prestigious institutions, including MIT's Draper Labs, Cisco Systems, and Raytheon, where he served as a technical lead for the Electromagnetic Environmental Effects Group. Yet despite a career surrounded by the brightest minds in technology and innovation, Ron's deepest passion has always been the universal life-force energy that underlies all things.

His journey into the unseen began at age sixteen with the disciplined practice of martial arts, where he would go on to earn master's ranks across multiple systems. That passion expanded into the study of Chinese qigong and taiji, opening the door to energy-based approaches to health, balance, and transformation.

A pivotal moment in Ron's life followed a catastrophic event that led him to explore the deeper worlds of energy healing, shamanic wisdom, and mind science. There, through sacred traditions once used to dissolve poverty, illness, and human conflict, Ron found the missing links that unified his scientific knowledge with spiritual truth.

In a moment of profound clarity, Ron synthesized these worlds into a single, coherent system: Master the Science of Miracles®. This work is the embodiment of his life's quest—to show others how the forces once wielded by sages and shamans can now be understood, harnessed, and applied by anyone seeking to turn vision into reality.

Ron now devotes his time to guiding others on the same path, blending the best of ancient spiritual insight with scientific rigor. His work is an invitation to remember your inherent power, and to discover for yourself how thoughts—when properly energized—can become miracles in motion.

Ready to take the next step?

Visit www.MasterTheScienceOfMiracles.com to join the community, explore programs, or schedule a breakthrough session.

www.ingramcontent.com/pod-product-compliance
Lightning Source LLC
Chambersburg PA
CBHW031945080426
42735CB00007B/271